Holt Spanish Level 1

# ¡Ven conmigo!®

## Practice and Activity Book

## Teacher's Edition

**with Overprinted Answers**

HOLT, RINEHART AND WINSTON
*Harcourt Brace & Company*
**Austin** • New York • Orlando • Atlanta • San Francisco • Boston • Dallas • Toronto • London

## Contributing Writers:

Jean Miller
Dana Todd





**Cover Photo/Illustration Credits**
Group of students: Marty Granger/HRW Photo; backpack/books: Sam Dudgeon/HRW Photo
All other photos are HRW photos by Marty Granger/Edge Productions.





Printed in the United States of America

ISBN 0-03-052603-5

3 4 5 6 7 021 03 02 01 00

# Contents

# *To the Teacher*

Contextualized practice is one of the most important steps on the road to achieving language proficiency. The *Practice and Activity Book* is filled with opportunities for students to practice the newly learned functions, grammar, and vocabulary in lifelike contexts. A variety of formats make the activities appealing and ensure that students will be able to use their new language skills in a wide range of situations.

Each chapter of the *Practice and Activity Book* provides the following types of practice.

**De antemano**
Brief recognition-based activities reinforce newly introduced concepts.

**Primer, segundo, and tercer pasos**
Multiple activities practice functions, grammar, and vocabulary. These include structured practice and transitional, guided practice, as well as more creative, open-ended work.

**Vamos a leer**
Additional reading selections and comprehension activities give students opportunities to practice the reading strategies, vocabulary, and skills taught in the chapter.

**Cultura**
This section offers several opportunities for students to reinforce the newly acquired cultural information from the chapter.

**En mi cuaderno**
Additional journal activities on pages 145–156 give students the opportunity to apply the writing strategies they learned, in relevant, personalized contexts.

Answers to all activities are included in the *Practice and Activity Book, Teacher's Edition*. Annotations in the *Annotated Teacher's Edition* suggest appropriate uses and applications of the *Practice and Activity Book.*

Nombre ______________________ Clase ____________ Fecha ____________

# ¡ADELANTE!

**1** How would you respond to each of the following questions or statements? First, write in the missing Spanish punctuation marks. Then, write your responses and practice them aloud.

¿Cómo te llamas?

¡Buenos días!

¿Cómo se dice "I have a question" en español?

1. **Me llamo...**
2. **Buenos días.**
3. **Tengo una pregunta.**

¿Cómo se escribe *burro*?

¡Buenas tardes!

¿XrüxKi?

4. **Se escribe b-u-r-r-o.**
5. **Buenas tardes.**
6. **¿Puede repetir, por favor?**
   **No entiendo; No sé.**

**2** Unscramble each of the following words to reveal the name of a Spanish-speaking country. Refer to the maps on pages xxiv and xxv of your textbook if you need help.

1. RHNOUASD **HONDURAS**
2. ZLAEVUEEN **VENEZUELA**
3. ELCHI **CHILE**
4. MÁNPAA **PANAMÁ**
5. GANTIENAR **ARGENTINA**
6. TUGMLAEAA **GUATEMALA**
7. ARANGCIAU **NICARAGUA**
8. YUGRUAU **URUGUAY**
9. MOBICLOA **COLOMBIA**
10. LE AVSLDOAR **EL SALVADOR**
11. GRAUYAPA **PARAGUAY**
12. DOCUREA **ECUADOR**
13. TOASC ICAR **COSTA RICA**
14. LVOBIIA **BOLIVIA**
15. RÚPE **PERÚ**

Nombre ______________________ Clase ______________ Fecha ______________

**3** When you travel in a Spanish-speaking country you'll have to know how to fill out forms with your name and address. Answer the following questions. **Answers will vary.**

1. ¿Cómo se escribe tu nombre completo? ______________________
2. ¿Cómo se escribe el nombre de tu calle *(street)*? ______________________
3. ¿Cómo se escribe el nombre de tu ciudad *(city)*? ______________________
4. ¿Cómo se escribe el nombre de tu estado *(state)*? ______________________

**4** Imagine that you're mixing paints. What two colors would you mix to get the following results? Be sure to include the definite article **el** *(the)* with each color.

1. **el rojo** + **el azul** = el morado
2. **el rojo** + **el amarillo** = el anaranjado
3. **el azul** + **el amarillo** = el verde
4. **el rojo** + **el blanco** = el rosado
5. **el blanco** + **el negro** = el gris

**5** Use the Spanish words you've been learning to fill out the following crossword puzzle.

**Horizontales** *(Across)*

4. country in Central America, just north of Costa Rica
6. country in South America, between Chile and Uruguay
10. veinticinco – ocho = ______
11. Spanish boy's name, Nacho for short
12. cherries are this color
13. ocho – siete = ______

**Verticales** *(Down)*

1. chocolate is this color
2. diecisiete – trece = ______
3. veintiséis – once = ______
4. doce – tres = ______
5. broccoli is this color
7. rojo + blanco = ______
8. veintidós + ocho = ______
9. ______ + azul = verde

Nombre ______________________ Clase ______________ Fecha ______________

# ¡Mucho gusto!



## DE ANTEMANO

**1** Look at the letter that Mercedes sent to Paco on page 19 of your textbook. Use the words and phrases in the box to write a short introduction for each of the two students shown below.

**Soy de... Me llamo... Tengo ... años. Me gusta...**

Juan Carlos/
San Sebastián/
16 años/
el voleibol

**Me llamo Juan Carlos.**

**Soy de San Sebastián.**

**Tengo 16 años.**

**Me gusta el voleibol.**

María Ángeles/
Santo Domingo/
14 años/
la pizza

**Me llamo María Ángeles.**

**Soy de Santo Domingo.**

**Tengo 14 años.**

**Me gusta la pizza.**

**2** Now look carefully at how Paco and his friends greet one another. Choose words and phrases from the box to complete the following dialogues. Use each word or phrase only once.

**Excelente, gracias. ¿Y tú? Adiós. Buenos días. ¡Hola! ¿Qué tal?**

1. PACO Hasta luego, María.
   MARÍA **Adiós.**
2. JAVIER **Buenos días.**
   CONSUELO Hola, Javier. ¿Qúe tal?
3. MARTA Hola, Gerardo. ¿Cómo estás?
   GERARDO **Excelente, gracias. ¿Y tú?**
4. PABLO **¡Hola! ¿Qué tal?**
   FERNANDO Muy bien, Pablo, ¿y tú?

Nombre ______________________ Clase ____________ Fecha ____________

# PRIMER PASO

**3** Match each of the following short conversations with the pictures. Write in the blank the letter of the picture that corresponds to the conversation.

a.

b.

c.

__c__ 1. — Bueno, tengo que irme. Hasta luego.

— ¡Chao!

__a__ 2. — Buenas tardes, señora Sánchez.

— Hola, Marisa.

__b__ 3. — Buenas noches, señorita Martínez.

— Buenas noches, Carlos.

**4** Write the letter of an appropriate response in the blank next to each statement or question. Some responses may be used more than once.

| If someone said . . . | A logical response would be . . . |
|---|---|
| __c__ 1. ¿Cómo te llamas? | **a.** Adiós. |
| __d *or* e__ 2. Éste es Felipe. | **b.** Igualmente. |
| __b *or* e__ 3. Encantado. | **c.** Me llamo Conchita. |
| __a *or* g__ 4. Hasta luego. | **d.** Encantado. |
| __d *or* e__ 5. Me llamo Conchita. | **e.** Mucho gusto. |
| | **f.** ¡Hola! |
| | **g.** Hasta luego. |

**5** A number of people have just been asked **¿Cómo estás?** First, punctuate the phrases and add any missing accents. Then match each of their responses with the letter of the drawing that best expresses how each person is doing.

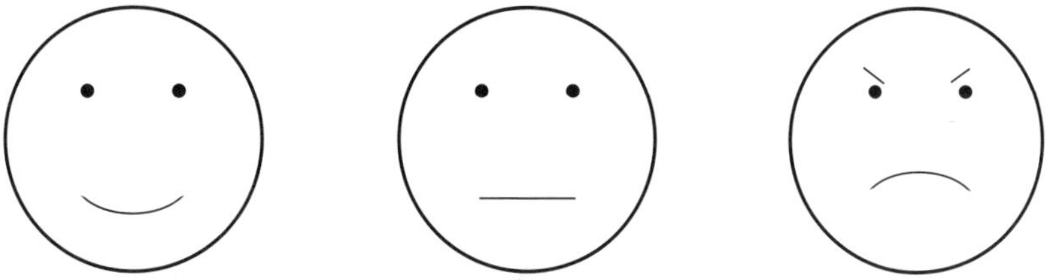

a. b. c.

a 1. ¡Estoy excelente!

b 2. Estoy regular.

b *or* a 3. Bien, gracias.

c 4. Estoy muy mal.

a 5. Estoy muy bien.

a 6. ¡Estupendo!

b 7. Más o menos.

b 8. Regular, ¿y tú?

**6** You have learned several phrases to say hello, to introduce yourself, to ask someone's name, to ask how someone feels, and to tell how you feel. Match these phrases to one of the two pictures of Teresa, according to whether she is talking about herself or talking to you.

a.

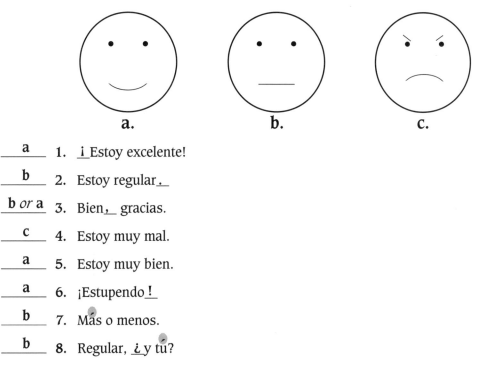

b.

a 1. Me llamo Teresa.

a 2. Encantada.

b 3. Hasta mañana.

a 4. Estoy bien.

b 5. ¿Qué tal?

a 6. Estoy regular.

b 7. ¿Cómo estás?

a 8. Yo soy Teresa.

Nombre ____________ Clase ____________ Fecha ____________

**7** Read the numbered phrases or questions below and decide which statement (**a** to **f**) applies to each one. Follow the **modelo**.

I should use this phrase . . .

**a.** to find out information
**b.** to greet someone
**c.** to introduce myself
**d.** when I have just met someone
**e.** to say goodbye to someone
**f.** to introduce someone else

MODELO __e__ **Adiós.**

__b__ 1. Hola.

__c__ 2. Yo soy...

__e__ 3. Hasta luego.

__d__ 4. Encantado/a.

__c__ 5. Yo me llamo...

__b__ 6. Buenas tardes.

__f__ 7. Ésta es...

__a__ 8. ¿Cómo te llamas?

__d__ 9. Igualmente.

__d__ 10. Mucho gusto.

**8** It's the first day of school, so there are a lot of people meeting each other for the first time! For each of the following pictures, fill in the blanks to complete the conversations.

1. MARTÍN Hola. **¿Cómo te llamas?**
NURIA Me llamo Nuria.
MARTÍN Y yo soy Martín.
2. NURIA **Mucho gusto, Martín.**
____________
MARTÍN Igualmente.

3. LUCILA **Éste es Jesús.**
____________
MANUEL Hola, Jesús. Mucho gusto.
4. JESÚS **Igualmente; Mucho gusto; Encantado. ¿Cómo estás?**
5. MANUEL Bien, gracias, ¿y **tú**?

Nombre ______________________ Clase __________ Fecha __________



# SEGUNDO PASO

**9** Write out these math problems following the **modelo**.

MODELO 2 + 8 = **Dos y ocho son diez.**

1. 4 + 15 = **Cuatro y quince son diecinueve.**
2. 12 + 3 = **Doce y tres son quince.**
3. 6 + 20 = **Seis y veinte son veintiséis.**
4. 11 + 13 = **Once y trece son veinticuatro.**
5. 27 + 1 = **Veintisiete y uno son veintiocho.**
6. 14 + 16 = **Catorce y dieciséis son treinta.**

**10** Look at each of the illustrations below. Write a sentence telling the age of each of the people shown.

1. Cristina 2. Rodolfo 3. Leonardo 4. Silvia 5. tú

1. **Cristina tiene un año.**
2. **Rodolfo tiene catorce años.**
3. **Leonardo tiene cuatro años.**
4. **Silvia tiene veintiún años.**
5. **Yo tengo ... años.**

**11** School has just started, and two new students, Pilar and Verónica, are talking about some of the people they've met so far. Complete their conversation by filling in the missing forms of the verbs **tener** and **ser**.

PILAR ¿Cuántos años **tiene** Marcos?

VERÓNICA Dieciséis años.

PILAR ¿Y tú, Verónica? ¿Cuántos años **tienes**?

VERÓNICA Yo **tengo** quince años.

PILAR ¿Sí? Yo también. Oye, Vero, ¿de dónde **eres** tú?

VERÓNICA **Soy** de Monterrey, México.

PILAR ¡Yo también! ¿Y Matilde?

VERÓNICA Matilde **es** de Santa Fe de Bogotá, Colombia.

**12** Choose the correct question word to complete the conversations.

cuántos · cómo · dónde

MARÍA Buenos días, Antonio. ¿ **Cómo** estás?

ANTONIO Estoy bastante bien, gracias.

PEDRO ¿De **dónde** es Jean?

JULIA Es de los Estados Unidos.

ANA ¿ **Cómo** se llama él?

CARLOS Se llama Juanito.

ESTEBAN Oye, Irene, ¿ **cuántos** años tiene Pablo?

IRENE Tiene catorce años.

**13** Mike is a seventeen-year-old exchange student from Michigan living in Madrid. On his first day of classes Maribel strikes up a conversation. Fill in Mike's half of the conversation.

**Answers will vary. Possible answers:**

1. MARIBEL Hola, soy Maribel. ¿Cómo te llamas tú?
   MIKE **Me llamo Mike.**
2. MARIBEL Encantada, Mike.
   MIKE **Igualmente.**
3. MARIBEL Tú no eres de Madrid, ¿verdad? ¿**De dónde eres**?
   MIKE Soy de los Estados Unidos.
4. MARIBEL ¿Y cuántos años tienes?
   MIKE **Tengo diecisiete años.**
5. MARIBEL Bueno, Mike, tengo que irme. ¡Chao!
   MIKE **¡Hasta luego!**

Nombre ______________________ Clase ____________ Fecha ____________



# TERCER PASO

**14** Whatever Beto likes, Memo doesn't like, and whatever Memo likes, Beto doesn't—except for one thing! Fill in the missing parts of each boy's statements according to the pictures.

**Beto**

**Memo**

1. BETO ¿ **Qué te** gusta?
   MEMO A mí **no me gusta** el tenis.
2. BETO **Me** gusta el fútbol norteamericano.
   MEMO A mí **no me gusta** el fútbol norteamericano.
3. BETO ¿ **Te gusta** la natación?
   MEMO A mí **me gusta** mucho la natación.
   BETO Pues a mí no me gusta **la natación**.
4. BETO **No me gusta** el béisbol.
   MEMO Pues a mí **me gusta** el béisbol.
5. BETO **Me gusta** el baloncesto.
   MEMO ¡A mí también!

**15** Read the following short interview between *Estrella* magazine and Juanito Serrano, a young pop singer. Complete the interview by filling in the blanks with either **el** or **la**.

**E** Juanito, ¿qué te gusta?

**JS** ¿Qué me gusta? Bueno, me gusta un poco de todo *(a little bit of everything)*.

**E** ¿Te gusta **la** pizza?

**JS** Sí, me gusta, pero me gusta más **la** comida china. ¡Y **el** chocolate!

**E** ¿Y los deportes?

**JS** Bueno, me gusta **el** baloncesto, y también **la** natación. No me gusta **el** voleibol.

**E** ¿Qué más? *(What else?)*

**JS** Bueno, me gusta mucho **la** música rock y clásica. Y **la** clase de inglés me gusta mucho también, pero no me gusta **la** tarea.

Nombre ______________________ Clase ____________ Fecha ____________

**16 a.** For each category given below, choose an item that you like and write a sentence saying that you like it. Then choose another item and write a sentence saying that you don't like it. Be sure to write **el** or **la** in front of the name of each item.

**la natación** **la tarea** **la comida italiana** **el fútbol** **la música rock** **la ensalada** **el béisbol** **el chocolate** **la música clásica** **el español** **la clase de inglés** **el jazz**

**Answers will vary. Some possible answers:**

La música: **Me gusta la música clásica. No me gusta el jazz.**

La comida: **Me gusta la comida italiana. No me gusta la ensalada.**

Los deportes: **Me gusta el béisbol. No me gusta el fútbol.**

Las clases: **Me gusta el español. No me gusta la tarea.**

**b.** Look at the box and write a question asking a friend what he or she likes. Then write your friend's answer.

**Possible answer: ¿Te gusta el jazz?**

**Me gusta el jazz.**

**17** Heather is practicing her Spanish with Antonio, the new exchange student from Spain. Based on Antonio's answers, supply the questions Heather asked him.

HEATHER **¿Cómo te llamas?**

ANTONIO Me llamo Antonio Carreras Llosa.

HEATHER **¿Cómo estás?**

ANTONIO Estoy bien, gracias.

HEATHER **¿Cuántos años tienes?**

ANTONIO Tengo diecisiete años.

HEATHER **¿De dónde eres?**

ANTONIO Soy de Barcelona, España.

**18** You've just gotten a pen pal from Spain, Maricarmen Martínez García. Write her a short letter. Tell her about yourself: your name, how you are, how old you are, where you're from, and what you like and don't like. Close your letter by saying goodbye. Be sure to ask your pen pal questions about herself too. (Begin your letter **Querida Maricarmen**, *Dear Maricarmen,*)

# VAMOS A LEER

**19** Imagine that your pen pal Maricarmen has sent you a reply to your first letter. Read her letter, then answer the following questions.

*Hola,*

*Muchas gracias por tu carta tan agradable. Ya sabes que me llamo Maricarmen. Pues, ¿sabes mis apellidos? Soy Maricarmen Martínez García. Tengo quince años y soy estudiante. Soy de Madrid. Madrid es la capital de España y es una ciudad maravillosa. Me gusta Madrid porque siempre hay muchas cosas interesantes que hacer. También me gusta el fútbol. No me gusta el fútbol norteamericano. ¡Es difícil de entender! Pero sí me gusta la música norteamericana. La música pop es estupenda, ¿sabes? Tengo varios discos compactos de Jewel, U2 y REM. También me gustan las películas de Hollywood. La actriz norteamericana que más me gusta es Sandra Bullock. También me gusta el actor Tom Cruise. Bueno, espero recibir una carta tuya muy pronto. ¡Hasta luego!*

*Tu amiga*
*Maricarmen*

1. List the names of any places you can find in the letter above.
   **Madrid; España; Hollywood**
2. List any names of sports you can find.
   **el fútbol; el fútbol norteamericano**
3. List at least three things that Maricarmen likes.
   **Madrid; el fútbol; la música norteamericana; las películas de Hollywood**
4. List one thing Maricarmen doesn't like.
   **el fútbol norteamericano**
5. Judging from its context, what do you think the word **películas** means?
   **movies**
6. What do you have in common with Maricarmen?
   **Answers will vary.**

Nombre ______________________ Clase ____________ Fecha ____________

# CULTURA

**20** Typically, people in Spanish-speaking countries have a **nombre** *(first name)* and two **apellidos** *(last names)*. Where do those last names come from? Here is Maricarmen's family tree, complete with all the **nombres** and **apellidos** of her parents and grandparents. Look at the names in the family tree, then answer the questions.

Juan Carlos Martínez Gómez — María Elena Blanco de Martínez

Lorenzo García Vázquez — Isabel Torres de García

Vicente Martínez Blanco

Mariano Martínez Blanco — Soledad García Torres (de Martínez)

Maricarmen Martínez García

1. What is Maricarmen's father's full name? **Mariano Martínez Blanco**
2. What is Maricarmen's uncle's full name? **Vicente Martínez Blanco**
3. What is Maricarmen's mother's full name? **Soledad García Torres (de Martínez)**
4. Which names did Maricarmen take from each of her parents? **Martínez García**
5. If you were to go to Madrid, and wanted to call up Maricarmen, what name would you look under in the Madrid phone book? **Martínez García**

**21** **a.** Spanish-speaking people greet each other differently than many people in the United States. Decide whether the following statements are **cierto** *(true)* or **falso** *(falso)*.

1. **c** Friends in Spain often greet each other with a kiss on both cheeks.
2. **f** Like Spaniards, Latin Americans kiss each other on both cheeks when saying hello.
3. **c** Young people in Spanish-speaking countries often shake hands when meeting or when saying goodbye.
4. **f** Spanish-speaking men only shake hands when greeting one another.
5. **f** In Spanish-speaking cultures, family members usually greet each other with a handshake.

**b.** How do you, your family, and your friends normally greet each other? How is this different from the way Spanish-speakers customarily greet each other? Is one more "formal" than the other? more "friendly"? How far apart do you stand or sit from each other?

**Answers may vary.**

CAPÍTULO 2

Nombre ______________________ Clase ______________ Fecha ______________

# ¡Organízate!

## DE ANTEMANO

**1** You're a clerk at the school store, and one of your customers asks you to help him check his bill. Next to each price on the ticket, write the item it represents.

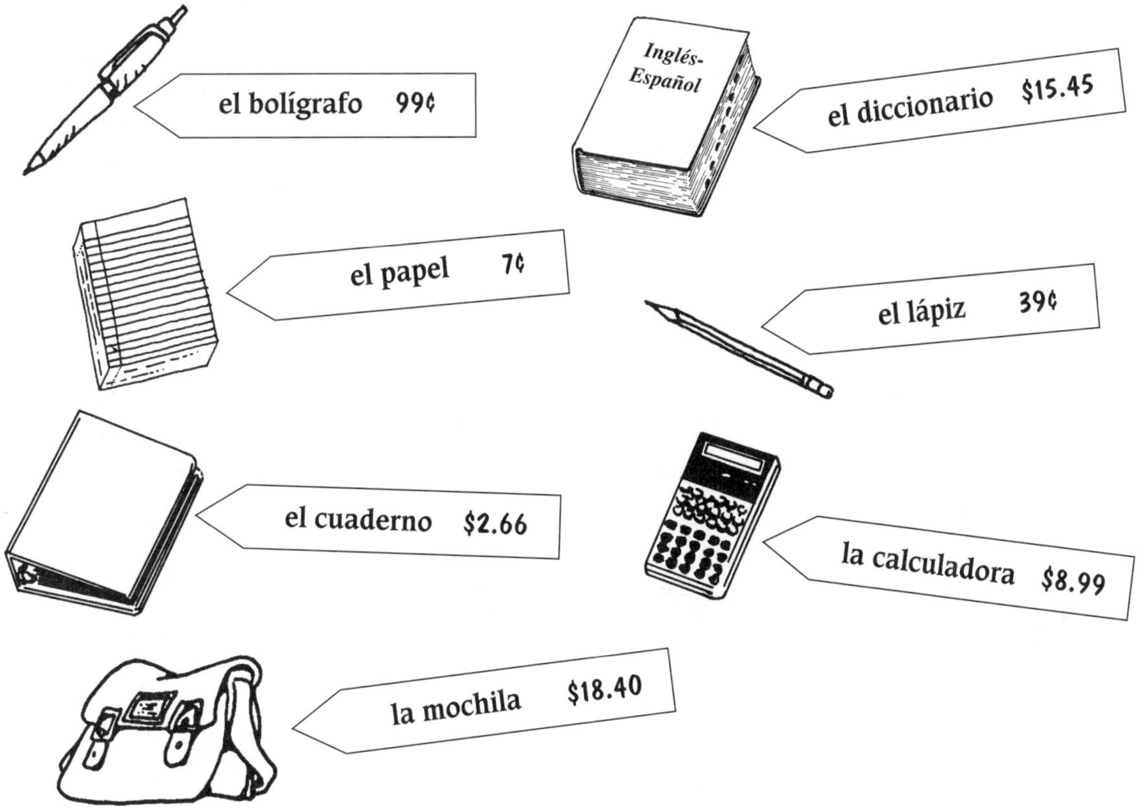


**2** It's the first day of classes and the bookstore is crowded. You overhear the following conversations. Can you match each question and answer?

__e__ 1. ¿Qué necesitas?

__a__ 2. ¿Tienes una calculadora?

__d__ 3. ¿Necesitas cuadernos?

__f__ 4. ¿Tienes papel?

__g__ 5. ¿Tienes zapatillas de tenis?

__c__ 6. ¿Necesitas más bolígrafos?

__b__ 7. ¿Ya tienes una mochila?

**a.** Sí, ya tengo una calculadora.
**b.** No, no tengo mochila.
**c.** No, ya tengo muchos bolígrafos.
**d.** No, no necesito cuadernos. Ya tengo tres.
**e.** ¡Ay, necesito muchas cosas!
**f.** No, no tengo papel. Necesito papel y también unos lápices.
**g.** Sí, tengo unas zapatillas de tenis.

# PRIMER PASO

**3** The Librería San Martín will give away a year's supply of pens to the first customer to complete this crossword puzzle. Write in the Spanish words for the items pictured below. Include the correct definite article with each item.

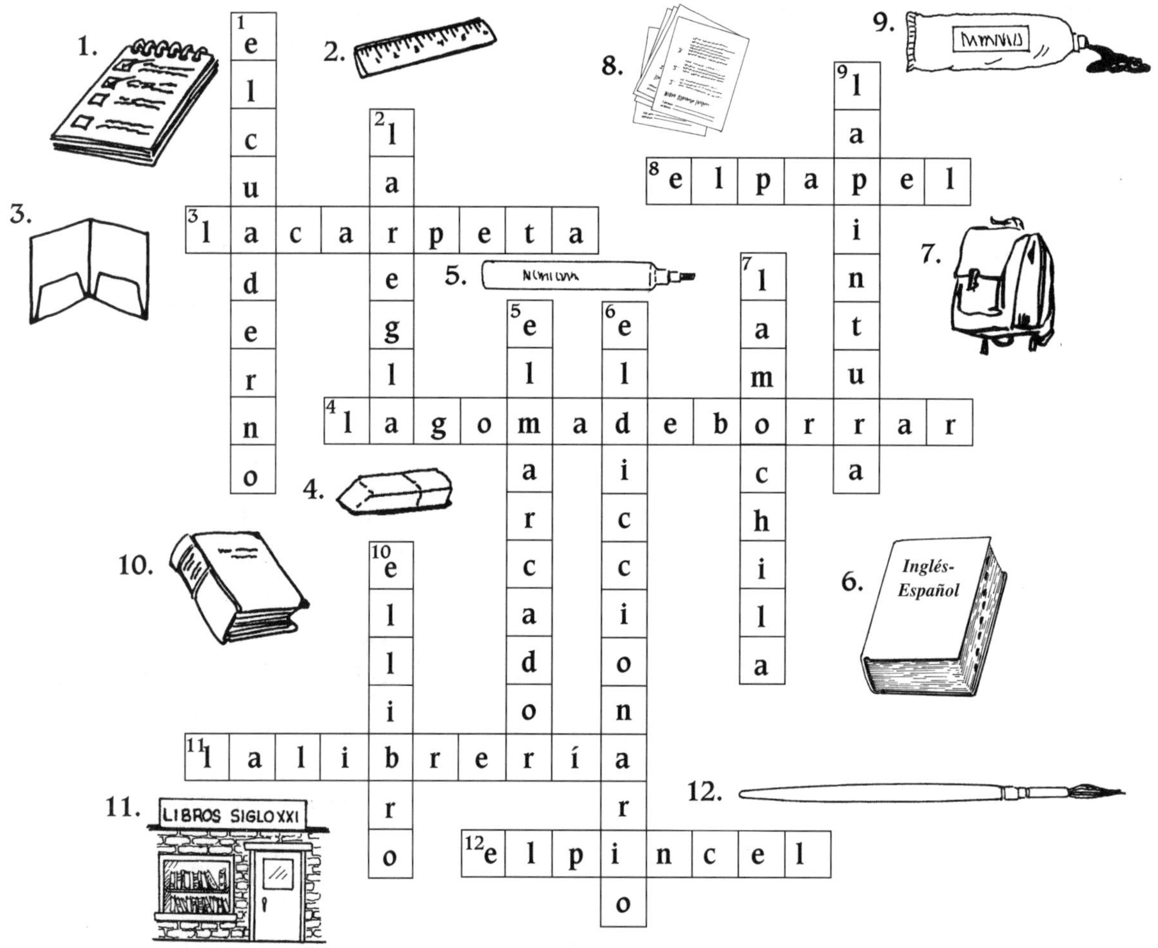


**4** Complete the conversation between Guillermo and the bookstore clerk with the correct indefinite articles (**un** or **una**) and the word for each item pictured.

DEPENDIENTE Hola, buenos días. ¿Qué necesita? 

GUILLERMO Hola. Por favor, necesito **un bolígrafo**.

DEPENDIENTE Muy bien. ¿Algo más? 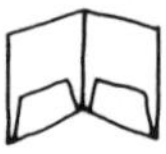 

GUILLERMO Sí. Necesito **una carpeta**, **un cuaderno** y **una regla**. 

DEPENDIENTE ¡Necesita muchas cosas! 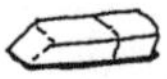 

GUILLERMO Sí. También necesito **una goma de borrar**, **una mochila** y  **una calculadora**. ¡Y ahora necesito dinero!

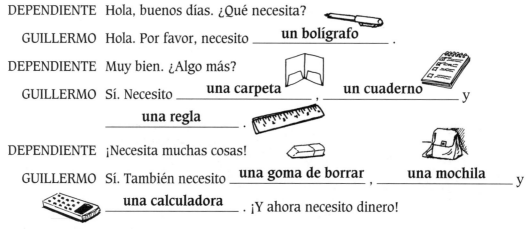

Nombre ______________________ Clase ______________ Fecha ______________

**5** Imagine that you're in the bookstore below and you need four different items. Complete the conversation you might have with the clerk. **Answers may vary. Possible Answers:**

SRTA. SOLER Buenas tardes. ¿Qué **necesitas** ?

TÚ Necesito un **libro** y una **goma de borrar** , por favor.

SRTA. SOLER ¿Ya tienes **una mochila** ?

TÚ Sí, pero no tengo **un diccionario** .

SRTA. SOLER ¿Quieres **algo más** ?

**6** Choose four of the students in the illustration above. For each one, write a question asking what the student wants or needs. Then answer the question. In your answers, use **él** and **ella** instead of the customer's names.

MODELO **¿Qué necesita Teresa? Ella necesita papel.**

1. (necesitar) **Possible answers: ¿Qué necesita Horacio?**
   **Él necesita una calculadora.**
2. (necesitar) **¿Qué necesita Lourdes?**
   **Ella necesita un diccionario.**
3. (querer) **¿Qué quiere Amalia?**
   **Ella quiere una regla y una mochila.**
4. (necesitar) **¿Qué necesita Martín?**
   **Él necesita un cuaderno.**

**7** You work in the lost-and-found office at school and someone has just turned in a lost bookbag. Fill out a report by describing the contents. Mention at least ten school supplies

MODELO **En la mochila hay una regla. También hay...**

**Answers may vary. Possible answers: En la mochila hay unos bolígrafos y también unos lápices. Hay un diccionario y una regla. También hay un pincel y unos marcadores. Hay una calculadora y un cuaderno. Y hay papel, unos libros y unas carpetas.**

**8** You just got a new job at a bookstore. The store is overstocked with school supplies and you've got to try to sell them all. Use all the words from the box to make questions asking your customers what they need. Be sure to use the formal **usted** with your customers. Don't forget to include the proper indefinite article when necessary.

| | | | | | |
|---|---|---|---|---|---|
| diccionario | calculadora | | papel | regla | cuadernos |
| lápices | carpetas | gomas de borrar | libros | mochila | bolígrafos |

**Answers will vary. Possible Answers:**

**¿Ya tiene una calculadora?**

**¿Necesita unos cuadernos?**

**¿Quiere unos bolígrafos?**

Nombre ______________________ Clase ______________ Fecha ______________

# SEGUNDO PASO

**9** You have the opportunity to design your own bedroom! Look at the **Vocabulario** on pages 52 and 55 and decide on ten things you would like to have in your room. Then, write a short paragraph describing your new room. Make sure you say how many of each thing you would like to have.

**Answers will vary. Possible Answers:**

**En mi cuarto tengo dos camas, una lámpara, dos puertas, veinte revistas y tres teléfonos. Mi cuarto es grande y sofisticado. Tengo dos televisores, un armario y nueve carteles elegantes. También tengo un escritorio y dos sillas.**

**10** Fede and Juanjo are very different! List what each has in his room according to the drawing. Some words come from the **Un poco más . . .** box on page **52** of your textbook.

**En el cuarto de Fede, hay...**

**Answers may vary. Possible answers:**

**dos camas, una mesa y una ventana. También hay un estéreo y unos carteles. Hay ropa y una guitarra.**

**En el cuarto de Juanjo, hay...**

**una cama, pero no hay ventanas. Hay una computadora y un escritorio. Hay una silla. Hay un armario. Hay unas revistas también.**

**11** Your pen pal Lucila has just moved to a new city and has written a letter to you about her school, her classes, and her room in her new apartment. Complete her letter with the correct form of **mucho** or **cuánto.**

Querido amigo,

¡Hola! ¿Cómo estás? Yo estoy bien. Tengo **1.** **muchos** amigos aquí. **2.** ¿ **Cuántos** amigos tienes tú?

Mi colegio nuevo es muy grande, pero me gusta. Hay **3.** **muchos** estudiantes. **4.** ¿ **Cuántos** estudiantes hay en tu colegio? Tengo ocho clases. **5.** ¿ **Cuántas** clases tienes tú? Mi clase favorita es la clase de inglés. No hay **6.** **muchas** personas en la clase. **7.** ¿ **Cuántas** personas hay en tu clase de inglés? No me gusta la clase de álgebra. Es difícil. Hay **8.** **mucha** tarea y **9.** **muchos** exámenes. ¿Te gusta la clase de álgebra?

Vivo en un apartamento nuevo. Me gusta mucho mi cuarto. En mi cuarto, hay **10.** **muchas** ventanas. Y también tengo **11.** **muchos** carteles de mis actores favoritos. **12.** ¿ **Cuántos** hay en tu cuarto?

Bueno, necesito ir a la librería ahora. Necesito comprar **13.** **muchos** libros para mis clases. ¡Pero no tengo **14.** **mucho** dinero!

¡Hasta luego!

*Lucila*

CAPÍTULO 2 Segundo paso

**12** Write a letter back to Lucila, remembering to answer her questions. Include any other information you like about your school, your classes, or your room. Also, ask her what there is in her room and if she has a TV set.

*Querida Lucila,*

**Answers will vary. Possible Answers: ¿Qué hay en tu cuarto? ¿Tienes un televisor?**

*¡Hasta luego!*

**13** Flavia Martínez Campos is a new exchange student from Mexico at your school this year. There are a lot of things that she wants to know about school. Help her out by answering the following questions with full sentences.

MODELO FLAVIA ¿Cuántos profesores hay en el colegio?
TÚ **Hay treinta y un profesores en el colegio.**

1. ¿Cuántos estudiantes hay en tu clase de español?

   **Answers will vary.**

2. ¿Qué necesito para mi clase de inglés?

3. ¿Cómo se llama el director del colegio *(principal)*?

4. ¿Te gusta la comida de la cafetería? ¿Qué no te gusta?

5. ¿Hay comida mexicana en la cafetería? ¿Hay ensalada?

6. ¿Cuánta tarea hay en la clase de inglés?

7. ¿Necesito una calculadora?

8. ¿Tienes una mochila? Y yo, ¿necesito una mochila?

9. ¿Cuántos cuadernos necesito para las clases?

10. ¿Hay muchas revistas en español en la librería?

# TERCER PASO

**14** After school, you overhear a lot of different conversations going home on the bus. Can you match the questions with the answers?

__b__ 1. ¿Qué quieres hacer?

__c__ 2. ¿Necesitas comprar zapatillas de tenis?

__a__ 3. ¿Qué quiere hacer Paco?

__d__ 4. ¿Necesitas comprar muchas cosas en la librería?

**a.** Paco quiere ir al centro comercial.
**b.** Quiero ir a la pizzería. ¡La pizza es deliciosa!
**c.** Sí, necesito ir al centro comercial. Mis zapatillas son muy viejas.
**d.** Sí... necesito comprar de todo (*everything*). Pero no tengo mucho dinero.

**15** Look over the expressions in the **Así se dice** box on page 56 of your textbook. What phrase would you use to . . .?

1. ask a friend what he or she wants to do
**¿Qué quieres hacer?**

2. ask a customer in the bookstore what he or she needs to buy
**¿Qué necesitas comprar?**

3. tell a friend you need to organize your room
**Necesito organizar mi cuarto.**

4. tell a friend you don't want to do your homework
**No quiero hacer la tarea.**

5. tell your parent or guardian what school supplies you need
**Necesito...**

6. ask someone what Esteban wants to do
**¿Qué quiere hacer Esteban?**

7. say that you want to go to the pizzeria
**Quiero ir a la pizzería.**



**16** Carmen has just passed you a note in the hall about after-school plans, but part of the message is in code! Can you unscramble it and figure out what she's saying? Write the decoded version in the blanks beneath Carmen's note.

¡Laho! Necesito zgroiaran im tucaro, rpeo ieqrou ri la centro lmeocriac. Ncsoetie comprar cshuma socsa. ¿Uéq quieres chear út?

**Hola. Necesito organizar mi cuarto, pero quiero ir al centro comercial. Necesito comprar muchas cosas. ¿Qué quieres hacer tú?**

**17** It's the last period of the day, and everyone in Mr. Santos' class is thinking about after-school plans . . . including Mr. Santos! Answer the questions below about people's plans based on the drawing.

El profesor Santos | Rosaura | Matilde | Óscar | Eduardo | Julia | Sofía | Mateo

**Answers may vary somewhat. Possible answers are given.**

1. ¿Qué necesita hacer el profesor Santos?
   **El profesor Santos necesita organizar los papeles.**

2. ¿Qué necesita encontrar Rosaura?
   **Rosaura necesita encontrar el dinero.**

3. ¿Qué quiere comprar Óscar?
   **Óscar quiere comprar unas zapatillas de tenis.**

4. ¿Qué necesita hacer Julia?
   **Julia necesita poner la ropa en el armario.**

5. ¿Qué quiere hacer Mateo?
   **Mateo quiere ir a la pizzería.**

6. ¿Qué necesita comprar Matilde?
   **Matilde necesita comprar muchas cosas.**

7. ¿Qué necesita hacer Eduardo?
   **Eduardo necesita hacer la tarea para mañana.**

8. ¿Qué quiere hacer Sofía?
   **Sofía quiere ir al centro comercial.**

**18** It's been a while since Lupe has cleaned her room. Now she's got a lot of work ahead of her. Make a list of at least five things she needs to do, according to the drawing.

**Answers may vary somewhat. Possible answers include: Lupe necesita encontrar la zapatilla de tenis, poner la radio en la mesa, poner la lámpara en el escritorio, poner la ropa en el armario, encontrar el dinero, organizar los libros...**



**19** You've just finished helping out with the school inventory, and now it's time to report to your supervisor. Answer her questions about what's in the supply room according to the inventory sheet.

| | | | |
|---|---|---|---|
| libros | 81 | cuadernos | 92 |
| televisores | 12 | diccionarios | 41 |
| carteles | 59 | sillas | 61 |
| lámparas | 38 | escritorios | 77 |

MODELO ¿Cuántos libros hay?
**Hay ochenta y un libros.**

1. ¿Cuántos televisores hay? **Hay doce televisores.**
2. ¿Cuántas lámparas hay? **Hay treinta y ocho lámparas.**
3. ¿Cuántos cuadernos hay? **Hay noventa y dos cuadernos.**
4. ¿Cuántos diccionarios hay? **Hay cuarenta y un diccionarios.**
5. ¿Cuántas sillas hay? **Hay sesenta y una sillas.**
6. ¿Cuántos escritorios hay? **Hay setenta y siete escritorios.**
7. ¿Cuántos carteles hay? **Hay cincuenta y nueve carteles.**

Nombre ______________________ Clase ____________ Fecha ____________

# VAMOS A LEER

**20** You're waiting in line to buy your school supplies at the **Librería San Martín**, and it's taking forever. While you wait, look over the magazines on display, and see if you can answer the questions below.

a.

b.

c.

d.

ESTRELLAS
El cine en España
Las nuevas películas españolas
Películas chilenas
Entrevista con el director Mariano Cordero

Can you figure out what topics are covered in each magazine just by looking at the covers? Match each magazine to the topics below.

__b__ 1. Geography and travel

__c__ 2. Homemaking ideas

__d__ 3. Gossip about celebrities

__a__ 4. Sports

# CULTURA

**21** Juan Antonio, a student from Spain, will be coming to live with the McRae family for a whole year. The McRaes have two teenagers, Mike and Jennifer, and live in a house in a small town. While staying with them, Juan Antonio will have his own large room. He'll share a TV and a phone with Mike and Jennifer. Using what you've learned about many Spanish homes, what aspects of his life with the McRaes do you think will seem strange to Juan Antonio?

**Most Spaniards live in apartments, called *pisos*. Bedrooms are often smaller and brothers or sisters commonly share a room. Spanish families generally share one TV set and one telephone. With the McRaes, however, Juan Antonio is living in a house with his own large bedroom. The McRae children have their own TV set and their own phone.**

**22** Juan Antonio will be attending the local high school while he's living with the McRaes. After a week of school, he's writing a letter to his best friend back home. Keeping in mind what you learned about how life is in the Spanish-speaking world, what observations do you think Juan Antonio would make to his friend about high school in the United States?

**High school teachers in the U.S. generally stay in the same classrooms all day while the students change classrooms; in Spain, it's the other way around. High school students in the United States have lockers to keep their school supplies in, whereas in Spain students carry everything they need to and from school each day.**

CAPÍTULO 3

Nombre ______________________ Clase ______________ Fecha ______________

# Nuevas clases, nuevos amigos

## DE ANTEMANO

**1** As you know, it's Claudia's first day at her new school, and everybody—including Claudia—has lots of questions! See if you can match everybody's questions and answers in the columns below.

__c__ 1. ¿Cómo te llamas?

__d__ 2. ¿Cómo es el profesor Romanca?

__a__ 3. ¿Qué clase tienes a las ocho y cincuenta?

__f__ 4. ¿Cuándo es el descanso?

__b__ 5. ¿De dónde eres?

__e__ 6. ¿Cómo es la capital?

**a.** Yo tengo francés y Fernando tiene geografía.
**b.** Soy del Distrito Federal.
**c.** Me llamo María Inés. Encantada.
**d.** Es aburrido. ¡No me gusta!
**e.** Es muy divertida. Hay muchas cosas interesantes allá (*there*). Me gusta mucho.
**f.** Es a las nueve y cuarenta.

**2** Match the following pictures with the comments.

1. __b__

2. __a__

3. __c__

**a.** A las ocho tengo francés, y a las nueve tengo la clase de ciencias sociales...
**b.** Mira, ya son las diez y media. Está atrasada la profesora.
**c.** ¡No me gustan las ciencias sociales!

Nombre ______________________ Clase ____________ Fecha ____________

# PRIMER PASO

**3** Use the pictures to fill in the classes that Ángela is taking this semester. Then rearrange the circled letters to find out what Ángela's favorite class is.

1. 

| | | | | | | | | |
|---|---|---|---|---|---|---|---|---|
| g | (e) | o | g | r | a | f | í | a |

2. 

| | | | |
|---|---|---|---|
| (a) | r | t | e |

3. 

| | | | | | | | | |
|---|---|---|---|---|---|---|---|---|
| e | d | u | c | a | c | (i) | ó | n |

| | | | | | |
|---|---|---|---|---|---|
| f | í | s | (i) | c | a |

4. 

| | | | | | | |
|---|---|---|---|---|---|---|
| f | r | a | n | (c) | é | s |

5. 

| | | | | | | | | | | |
|---|---|---|---|---|---|---|---|---|---|---|
| (c) | o | m | p | u | t | a | c | i | ó | (n) |

6. 

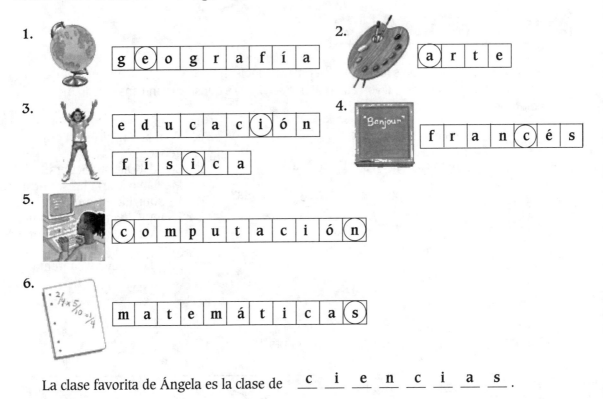

| | | | | | | | | | | |
|---|---|---|---|---|---|---|---|---|---|---|
| m | a | t | e | m | á | t | i | c | a | (s) |

La clase favorita de Ángela es la clase de c i e n c i a s.

**4** Look at Juan's class schedule, then complete his conversation with Mari using the words in the box.

mañana luego hoy por fin primero

| viernes | sábado |
|---|---|
| química | ¡LIBRE! |
| matemáticas | |
| alemán | |
| educación física | |
| almuerzo | |
| español | |
| computación | |

MARI Oye, Juan, ¿qué clases tienes **hoy**?

JUAN Bueno, **primero** tengo la clase de química. Después tengo **matemáticas**, **alemán** y **educación física**. **Luego** tengo el almuerzo, español, y **por fin** la clase de computación.

MARI ¿Y **mañana**? ¿Qué clases tienes?

JUAN Hombre, ¡el sábado es un día libre!

**5** Claudia is writing a short letter to her friend Sonia, back in Mexico City, about her life in Cuernavaca. Complete her letter with the correct definite article: **el**, **la**, **los**, or **las**.

*Cuernavaca*

*8 de octubre*

*Querida Sonia,*

*¿Cómo estás? Yo estoy muy bien aquí en Cuernavaca. Me gusta* 1. __el__ *nuevo colegio.* 2. __Los__ *estudiantes son simpáticos e inteligentes.* 3. __El__ *director se llama el Sr. Altamirano. Este año, tengo nueve materias.* 4. __Las__ *clases de ciencias sociales y literatura son mis favoritas. Son muy interesantes. También me gusta* 5. __la__ *clase de francés, pero necesito estudiar mucho.* 6. __Los__ *exámenes son difíciles. ¡Y* 7. __la__ *tarea es horrible! Bueno, ahora necesito ir a* 8. __la__ *librería. Quiero comprar* 9. __los__ *libros para* 10. __las__ *clases de geografía y biología. Después, voy a* 11. __la__ *pizzería con mis amigos Fernando y María Inés. ¡Escríbeme pronto!*

*Un abrazo,*

*Claudia*

**6** Teresa and Patricia were passing a note in study hall about their afternoon classes and plans for after school. Can you put the pieces of their torn-up note back in order? Write the number of the sentence in the left-hand column next to the sentence in the right-hand column that goes with it.

| | | | |
|---|---|---|---|
| 1. | *Hola, Tere. ¿Qué clases tienes?* | __2__ | *Sí, me gusta, pero necesito estudiar mucho. Hay mucha tarea.* |
| 2. | *¿Te gusta la clase?* | __5__ | *Sí, gracias. Necesito estudiar también.* |
| 3. | *Y después, ¿qué clases tienes?* | __1__ | *Bueno, primero tengo la clase de historia con el profesor Román.* |
| 4. | *Y después, ¿quieres ir al partido de basquetbol?* | __4__ | *Sí, quiero, pero necesito estudiar.* |
| 5. | *¿Quieres estudiar en mi casa?* | __3__ | *Después tengo computación, ciencias y luego español.* |

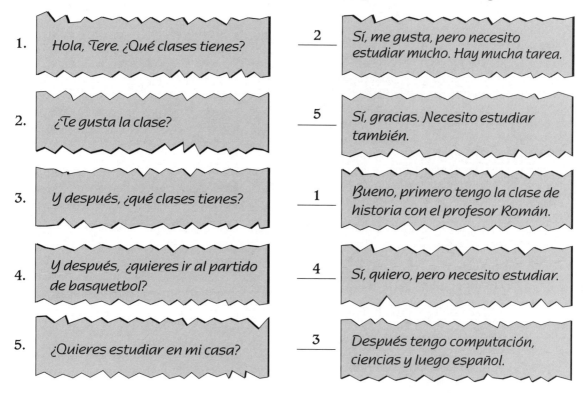

**7** On the first line below write a question asking what time it is. Then answer the question for each clock.

PREGUNTA **¿Qué hora es?**

1. **Son las doce y cuarto *or* Son las doce y quince.**
2. **Son las seis (en punto).**
3. **Son las siete y media.**

4. **Son las diez y cuarto *or* Son las diez y quince.**
5. **Son las tres menos veinte.**
6. **Es la una menos diez.**

**8** Look at the series of pictures showing a typical day in Esteban's life. What time do you think it is when Esteban does all these things? First number the drawings 1-4, according to the order in which they happen. Then write a sentence in Spanish saying what time you think it is in each drawing.

**2**

**3**

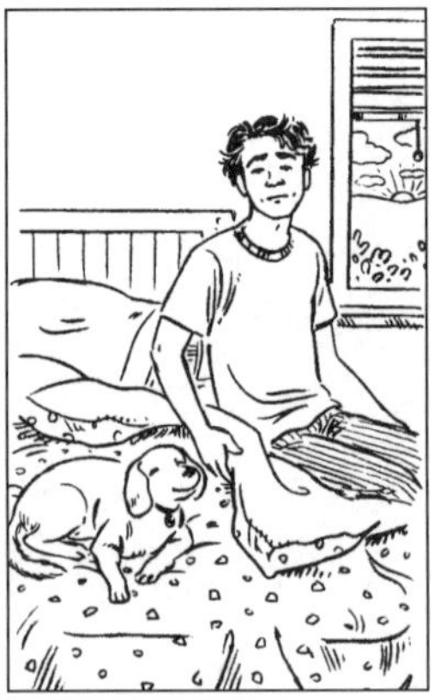

**1**

**4**

1. **Possible answers: Son las siete de la mañana.**
2. **Son las ocho y media de la mañana.**
3. **Son las doce en punto de la tarde.**
4. **Son las siete de la noche.**

# SEGUNDO PASO

**9** Beto and Lola are at the Pizzería Napolitana discussing the first day of classes. Complete their conversation with the words and expressions from the box. Some words or expressions may be used more than once.

| | | | | | | |
|---|---|---|---|---|---|---|
| prisa | es a las | ¿a qué hora es? | atrasada | a las | son las | ¿qué hora es? |

BETO ¿Qué clases tienes este semestre?

LOLA Bueno, primero tengo álgebra **a las** 8:45 de la mañana. Es una clase interesante. Después, **a las** 9:45 tengo geografía. Me gusta esa clase. Es divertida.

BETO Tengo geografía también, pero mi clase **es a las** 2:30 de la tarde. Mi clase favorita **es a las** 10:00 de la mañana. Es la clase de literatura. Hay mucha tarea en esa clase, pero me gusta.

LOLA Necesitas comprar muchos libros para la clase, ¿verdad?

BETO Sí. Necesito ir a la librería esta tarde **a las** seis.

LOLA Perdón, Beto... ¿**qué hora es** ahora?

BETO **Son las** cuatro y veinticinco.

LOLA ¡Es tarde! Estoy **atrasada**. Necesito ir a casa ahora mismo. Quiero ver (*to see*) mi programa de televisión favorito.

BETO ¿Y **a qué hora es** el programa?

LOLA ¡**Es a las** cuatro y media!

BETO Entonces, ¡date **prisa**!

**10** Bárbara's made a list of things she's going to do today and when she's going to do them. First decide whether each item in her list is something she wants to do or something she needs to do. Then write a sentence stating what she needs or wants to do and at what time. Write out the times, and indicate morning, afternoon, or evening, as in the model.

MODELO comprar lápices en la librería (3:00 P.M.)
**Bárbara necesita comprar lápices en la librería a las tres de la tarde.**

1. ir al colegio (8:45 A.M.)
   **Bárbara necesita/quiere ir al colegio a las nueve menos cuarto de la mañana.**

2. ir a la clase de español (9:50 A.M.)
   **Bárbara necesita/quiere ir a la clase de español a las diez menos diez de la mañana.**

3. ir a la pizzería (12:20 P.M.)
   **Bárbara necesita/quiere ir a la pizzería a las doce y veinte de la tarde.**

4. organizar el armario (3:30 P.M.)
**Bárbara necesita/quiere organizar el armario a las tres y media de la tarde.**

5. comprar nuevas zapatillas de tenis (4:15 P.M.)
**Bárbara necesita/quiere comprar nuevas zapatillas de tenis a las cuatro y cuarto de la tarde.**

6. hacer la tarea para mañana (6:00 P.M.)
**Bárbara necesita/quiere hacer la tarea para mañana a las seis en punto de la tarde.**

7. cenar (*to have dinner*) (8:15 P.M.)
**Bárbara necesita/quiere cenar a las ocho y cuarto de la noche.**

8. ir con los amigos a una fiesta (*party*) (9:40 P.M.)
**Bárbara quiere ir a una fiesta a las diez menos veinte de la noche.**

**11** Once again, Carmen's late for an appointment, this time with Professor Sánchez. Complete the following conversation between her and Felipe with the appropriate word from the box. You may use some words more than once.

qué hora | ahora | atrasada | prisa | atrasado | date | en punto | a qué hora

FELIPE Carmen, ¿por qué tienes 1. **prisa**?

CARMEN Es que estoy 2. **atrasada**.

FELIPE Pero, ¿por qué? Es temprano (*early*).

CARMEN Sí, pero necesito hablar (*to talk*) con el profesor Sánchez esta mañana.

FELIPE ¿De veras? 3. ¿**A qué hora** necesitas hablar con él?

CARMEN A las ocho 4. **en punto**. ¿Sabes (*Do you know?*) 5. **qué hora** es, Felipe?

FELIPE A ver. 6. **Ahora** son las ocho y cinco.

CARMEN ¡Ay, no! No puede ser. (*It can't be.*) Estoy muy 7. **atrasada**.

FELIPE Pues, no te preocupes (*don't worry*). El profesor Sánchez siempre está 8. **atrasado** también.

CARMEN Sí, pero ya está en su oficina (*He's already in his office*).

FELIPE 9. ¡**Date** prisa, Carmen! Hasta luego.

CARMEN Adiós.

Nombre ______________________ Clase ____________ Fecha ____________

**12** Rafael and Guillermo have run into each other in the hallway between classes. Write a short conversation between the two. Use the cues below as a guide.

| Rafael | Guillermo |
| --- | --- |
| Greets Guillermo. Asks him how he is. | Says fine, thanks, and asks about Rafael. |
| **Hola, Guillermo. ¿Cómo estás?** | **Bien gracias. ¿Y tú?** |
| Says he's so-so. Asks if Guillermo wants to go to the movies today. | Says yes, and asks at what time. |
| **Regular. ¿Quieres ir al cine hoy?** | **Sí. ¿A qué hora?** |
| Says at 4:30 P.M. | Says yes, he wants to go, but first he needs to do his homework. |
| **A las cuatro y media de la tarde.** | **Sí, quiero ir, pero necesito hacer la tarea primero.** |
| Says okay. Asks what time it is. | Says it's 2:30. Says he has class now. Says he's late. |
| **Está bien. ¿Qué hora es?** | **Son las dos y media. Tengo clase ahora. Estoy atrasado.** |
| Says he's late, too. Tells Guillermo to hurry up. | Says see you later. |
| **Yo también. ¡Date prisa, Guillermo!** | **Hasta luego.** |

**13** Claudia is having a difficult first week at her new school! She and Professor Garza just collided in the hallway, and now their stuff is all mixed up. Help sort things out by saying which things belong to which person, following the model below.

MODELO La regla / Claudia
**La regla es de Claudia.**

1. los exámenes / el profesor Garza **Los exámenes son del profesor Garza.**
2. las carpetas / Claudia **Las carpetas son de Claudia.**
3. el dinero / el profesor Garza **El dinero es del profesor Garza.**
4. el sándwich / Claudia **El sándwich es de Claudia.**
5. la fruta / el profesor Garza **La fruta es del profesor Garza.**
6. los libros / Claudia **Los libros son de Claudia.**
7. los bolígrafos / el profesor Garza **Los bolígrafos son del profesor Garza.**

Nombre ______________________ Clase ______________ Fecha ______________

# TERCER PASO

**14** Write a question for each illustration below using the tag question forms you learned on page 88 of your textbook. The first one is done for you as a model.

**mis amigos**

**Mis amigos son simpáticos, ¿verdad?**

**las clases**

**Las clases aquí son divertidas, ¿no?**

**los exámenes**

**Los exámenes son fáciles, ¿verdad?**

**el Presidente de EEUU**

**El Presidente de EEUU es alto, ¿no?**

**el monstruo**

**El monstruo es feo pero simpático, ¿no?**

**los profesores**

**Los profesores son nuevos, ¿verdad?**

**15** Claudia and Fernando are having a snack after class in a café. Complete their conversation with the correct forms of the verb **ser**.

FERNANDO Bueno, Claudia... ¿Cómo ___**son**___ tus clases?

CLAUDIA ¡Uf! ¡Ya tengo mucha tarea! Las clases ___**son**___ difíciles en este colegio.

FERNANDO Sí, aquí los profesores ___**son**___ muy estrictos.

CLAUDIA Mi profesor de computación se llama Profesor Guzmán.

FERNANDO ¡Ay! ¡Qué mala suerte! (*what rotten luck!*) Él ___**es**___ muy estricto.

CLAUDIA ¿Y cómo ___**es**___ la profesora de historia?

FERNANDO ¿La profesora Ureña? Bueno, ___**es**___ inteligente y divertida. Pero la clase no ___**es**___ fácil. Necesitas estudiar mucho.

CLAUDIA Y hay un profesor de biología... no sé cómo se llama. ___**Es**___ alto, guapo y moreno.

FERNANDO Ah, el profesor Chamorro. Es muy inteligente y la clase de biología ___**es**___ super-interesante.

CLAUDIA Bueno, tengo que irme. Necesito hacer la tarea para mañana.

FERNANDO Claudia, ¡no te preocupes (*Don't worry!*)! Tú ___**eres**___ muy inteligente.

**16** Complete the sentences below by circling the two adjectives that correctly match the subject of each sentence.

1. La profesora Alonso es...
   a. inteligentes (b.) baja c. moreno (d.) simpática
2. Las novelas de Mark Twain son...
   a. difícil (b.) cómicas (c.) interesantes d. aburrida
3. Mi amigo Roberto es...
   (a.) guapo b. cómica c. alta (d.) rubio
4. Las fiestas del club de español son...
   (a.) grandes b. aburrido (c.) divertidas d. buena
5. Los estudiantes de mi colegio son...
   a. bueno (b.) guapos (c.) inteligentes d. antipática
6. La clase de química es...
   a. interesantes b. fáciles (c.) divertida (d.) difícil
7. La tarea para mañana es...
   (a.) horrible b. divertidas c. fáciles (d.) aburrida
8. Mi perro (*dog*) Max es...
   a. malos (b.) cómico c. fea (d.) bonito

**17** Fill in the blanks of the sentences below with the correct form of the adjectives in parentheses.

1. Mi clase favorita es la geografía porque es **interesante** (interesante).
2. La profesora de español es muy **estricta** (estricto).
3. No me gustan las clases **aburridas** (aburrido).
4. Todos *(All)* mis amigos son **simpáticos** (simpático).
5. No me gustan los exámenes de matemáticas porque son **difíciles** (difícil).
6. Mi amiga Berta es **bonita** (bonito).

**18** Your little brother won't stop asking questions! Get him off your back by answering the questions below. Base your answers on your opinions of the things mentioned.

MODELO —¿Por qué te gusta la clase de español?
**—Me gusta porque es divertida.**

1. ¿Por qué no te gustan los exámenes?
   **Possible answers: No me gustan porque son difíciles.**
2. ¿Por qué te gustan los deportes?
   **Me gustan porque son divertidos.**
3. ¿Por qué te gustan los conciertos?
   **Me gustan porque son divertidos.**
4. ¿Por qué te gusta el profesor Román?
   **Me gusta porque es inteligente.**

**19** Your friends are very particular about their activities and don't like the same things you do. Explain how your interests differ from theirs using the model and the cues below.

MODELO Lisa / los videojuegos (no)
**A Lisa no le gustan los videojuegos. A mí me gustan.**

1. Pepe / la música pop (sí)
   **A Pepe le gusta la música pop. A mí no me gusta.**
2. Elena / las fiestas (no)
   **A Elena no le gustan las fiestas. A mí me gustan.**
3. Angélica / el colegio (sí)
   **A Angélica le gusta el colegio. A mí no me gusta.**
4. Paco / el dinero (no)
   **A Paco no le gusta el dinero. A mí me gusta.**
5. Carlota / los deportes (no)
   **A Carlota no le gustan los deportes. A mí me gustan.**

# VAMOS A LEER

**20** Do you have a favorite color? Do you think that someone's favorite color is an indication of his or her personality? Read the article below, then answer the questions. (HINT: If you've forgotten the colors, see page 9 of your textbook.)

## Analiza el "color" de tu personalidad

| | |
|---|---|
| Rojo | Si te gusta el rojo, entonces eres impulsivo(a), impaciente y extrovertido(a). |
| Azul | ¿Prefieres el azul? Pues, probablemente eres conservador(a), serio(a) e intelectual. |
| **Verde** | Si te gusta el verde, eres una persona paciente, generosa y tolerante. |
| Amarillo | El amarillo es el color de las personas optimistas e idealistas. Si prefieres el amarillo, probablemente eres muy activo(a) también. |
| **Anaranjado** | ¿Prefieres este color? Entonces eres sociable, realista y honesto(a). |
| Morado | Éste es el color de las personas artísticas, temperamentales y románticas. |

One of the reading strategies you've practiced is working with cognates (on page 36 of your textbook). You probably noticed some cognates as you were reading through this article. Find the Spanish cognates of these English adjectives:

| | | |
|---|---|---|
| honest | impulsive | serious |
| **honesto** | **impulsivo(a)** | **serio(a)** |
| generous | intellectual | active |
| **generoso(a)** | **intelectual** | **activo(a)** |
| temperamental | sociable | extroverted |
| **temperamental** | **sociable** | **extrovertido(a)** |

CAPÍTULO 3 Vamos a leer

# CULTURA

**21** People from the U.S. have a reputation in other countries for always being on time. Is that reputation true, or is it a stereotype? Is it ever all right to be late in this country? Make a list of three occasions when it's acceptable to arrive late, and three when it's necessary to be on time. Can you make any generalizations about your lists, and about attitudes towards time in the U.S.? How do your attitudes towards time differ from those in Spanish-speaking cultures?

**Answers will vary.**

**22** Below are some expressions you can use when someone tells you what grade he or she got:

**¡Qué bien!** *That's great!*
**Lo siento.** *I'm sorry.*

React to each student's comment about his or her grade using one of the expressions above. Base your reaction on what you learned about grading in Spanish-speaking countries.

MODELO Isabel(México, D.F.) Saqué (*I got*) un 10 en la clase de química.
Tú ¡Qué bien!

1. Gabriela (Oaxaca, México): Saqué un 8 en la clase de geometría.
   Tú: **¡Qué bien!**
2. Mariana (Lima, Perú): Saqué un 17 en la clase de inglés.
   Tú: **¡Qué bien!**
3. Felipe (Ciudad Juárez, México): Saqué un 5 en la clase de álgebra.
   Tú: **¡Lo siento!**
4. Daniela (Arequipa, Perú): Saqué un 12 en la clase de literatura.
   Tú: **¡Lo siento!**
5. Xóchitl (Jalisco, México): Saqué un 9 en la clase de computación.
   Tú: **¡Qué bien!**
6. José Alberto (Iquitos, Perú): Saqué un 19 en la clase de biología.
   Tú: **¡Qué bien!**

CAPÍTULO 4

Nombre ______________________ Clase ______________ Fecha ______________

# ¿Qué haces esta tarde?

## DE ANTEMANO

**1** As you saw in the **fotonovela**, everybody has a lot of questions. Match the different questions and answers below.

d 1. Luis, ¿vas a Taxco con Claudia y Rosa?

e 2. ¿Dónde está el correo?

a 3. ¿Qué hace María Inés después de bailar?

c 4. Claudia, tú cantas en el coro con María Inés, ¿verdad?

b 5. ¿A María Inés le gusta bailar?

a. Por lo general estudia en la biblioteca.

b. Sí, le gusta mucho. Los sábados baila con un grupo de baile folklórico.

c. No, Rosa. Canto en el coro con Luis.

d. Sí, señor... voy con ellas.

e. Está en la Plaza de la Constitución. ¿Vamos allá ahora?

**2** Complete Juan José's description of where he and his friends go and what they do after classes with one of the places below.

correo biblioteca librería centro comercial gimnasio cuarto casa

Después de clases hoy, voy al 1. **centro comercial**, porque quiero comprar unas zapatillas nuevas. Mi amiga Diana necesita ir a la 2. **biblioteca** para hacer la tarea para mañana. Ernesto va primero al 3. **correo**. Quiere comprar unas estampillas (*stamps*). Después va a 4. **casa** porque necesita organizar su 5. **cuarto**. Susana quiere jugar al voleibol en el 6. **gimnasio** con sus amigos. Y Cristóbal va a la 7. **librería** porque necesita comprar muchas cosas para las clases.

Nombre ______________________ Clase ______________ Fecha ______________

# PRIMER PASO

**3** Tomás is trying to find someone to shoot baskets with after classes. Complete his conversations with different classmates below with the expressions in the box. Each expression may be used more than once. Does Tomás find someone to play basketball with him?

| | |
|---|---|
| me gusta | te gusta |
| le gusta | qué haces |

TOMÁS José María, **1.** ¿ **qué haces** después de clases?

JOSÉ MARÍA Juego mucho al basquetbol. Es mi deporte favorito.

TOMÁS ¿Quieres jugar después de clases hoy?

JOSÉ MARÍA Necesito hacer la tarea, pero a Carmen **2.** **le gusta** jugar al basquetbol.

TOMÁS Carmen, **3.** **te gusta** el basquetbol, ¿no?

CARMEN ¿El basquetbol? Pues no, no **4.** **me gusta** . Me gusta el voleibol.

TOMÁS ¿El voleibol? Pero a mí no **5.** **me gusta** el voleibol.

CARMEN Pues habla (*talk*) con David. A él **6.** **le gusta** jugar al basquetbol.

TOMÁS Oye, David... 7. ¿ **te gusta** el basquetbol?

DAVID No, pero **8.** **me gusta** nadar. ¿Quieres nadar conmigo hoy después de clases?

TOMÁS No, gracias. ¡Quiero jugar al basquetbol!

DAVID Pues... a Luis **9.** **le gusta** practicar los deportes, sobre todo (*especially*) el basquetbol.

TOMÁS Ah, sí. Y a mí **10.** **me gusta** jugar con Luis. ¡Él juega (*plays*) muy bien! ¡Qué buena idea!

**4** Write a sentence for each picture, saying what the people in the drawings like and don't like to do.

1. 
Irina
**A Irina le gusta pintar.**

2. 
Felipe
**A Felipe le gusta escuchar música.**

3. 
César
**A César no le gusta sacar la basura.**

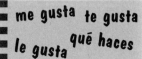

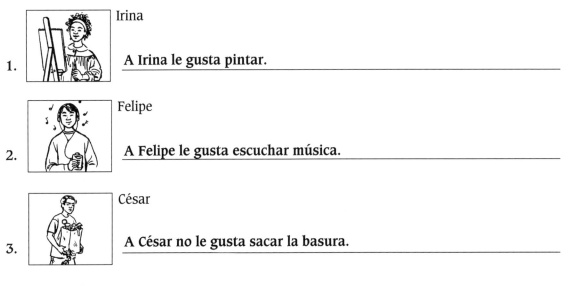

4. 
Fernanda

**A Fernanda le gusta descansar.**

5. 
Pedro

**A Pedro le gusta nadar.**

6. 
Sarita

**A Sarita no le gusta lavar la ropa.**

7. 
Juanita

**A Juanita le gusta mirar la televisión.**

**5** Write a letter to your friend Luis, who lives in Canada, and tell him what you do every day from first to last in the following places. Mention one or two activities you do with someone else. Be sure to use the words **primero, luego,** and **más tarde** to make your letter more interesting.

**en el colegio** **en casa** **en la cafetería** **en el parque** **en el centro comercial**

MODELO En el colegio...
**Primero, en el colegio, estudio. Luego, en la cafetería...**

*Querido Luis,*

**Possible Answer: Primero estoy en el colegio. En la cafetería, tomo un refresco. Luego, después de clases, me gusta descansar en el parque. Después, en casa, lavo la ropa, estudio y saco la basura. A las siete, estoy en el centro comercial y compro unas cosas que necesito. Por fin, en casa, mis amigos y yo escuchamos música y hablamos por teléfono con otros amigos.**

*Hasta Luego,*

Nombre ______________________ Clase ______________ Fecha ______________

**6** Look over the vocabulary section on pp. 101, 103 of your text, then complete the sentences below with the correct form of the missing verbs. Write the verbs in the correct space in the puzzle.

**HORIZONTALES**

Guillermo **2.** ___ la televisión por la tarde.
Mercedes y yo **4.** ___ en la clase de arte.
Nosotros **6.** ___ música en mi casa.
Yo siempre **10.** ___ a mi hermanito Luis.
Tú **11.** ___ con el perro todos los días, ¿verdad?
Javier y Gonzalo **12.** ___ la trompeta.
Pilar **13.** ___ el carro de su mamá.

**VERTICALES**

Rebeca **1.** ___ en un restaurante italiano.
Yo **3.** ___ un refresco con mis amigos.
Después de clases, Manolo **4.** ___ en su cuarto.
Mi papá y mi mamá **5.** ___ la cena.
Arturo e Isabel **7.** ___ en bicicleta en el parque.
Martín nunca **8.** ___ la basura.
Carolina **9.** ___ el piano.

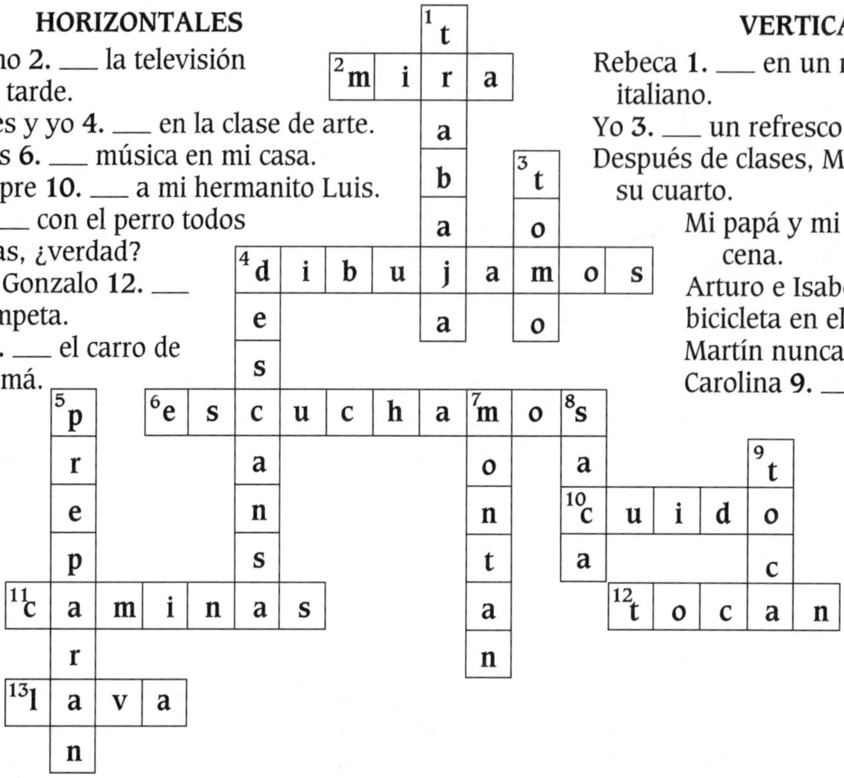


**7** Rosa's friend Héctor always wants to know what's going on. Write out Rosa's answers to Héctor's questions, using the cues in parentheses and following the model below.

MODELO HÉCTOR ¿Quién toma un refresco contigo? (Sara y Luis)
ROSA **Sara y Luis toman un refresco conmigo.**

1. ¿Quién monta en bicicleta conmigo? (Miguel y yo)
**Miguel y yo montamos en bicicleta contigo.**

2. ¿Quién trabaja en el restaurante con Susana? (Paco y Lupita)
**Paco y Lupita trabajan en el restaurante con Susana.**

3. ¿Quién nada con Sebastián y Carlota? (Enrique)
**Enrique nada con Sebastián y Carlota.**

4. ¿Quién mira la tele contigo? (Tú y Miguel)
**Tú y Miguel miran la tele conmigo.**

5. ¿Quién camina en el parque con Germán? (Yo)
**Yo camino en el parque con Germán.**

# SEGUNDO PASO

**8** Franco has just moved to a new town and is writing a letter describing it to his friend Rafael. Complete his letter with the correct form of the verb **estar**.

*Querido Rafa,*

*¿Cómo* 1. **estás** *, hombre? Yo* 2. **estoy** *muy bien. Me gusta mucho mi nueva ciudad. Mi casa* 3. **está** *en una zona muy bonita. El Parque de la Constitución* 4. **está** *muy cerca de la casa. ¡Hay una piscina muy grande en el parque! El colegio* 5. **está** *lejos. Necesito ir a clases en el autobús o el metro. Pero por suerte, la parada y la estación de metro* 6. **están** *al lado de mi casa. Mi colegio nuevo se llama Colegio Sarmiento, y* 7. **está** *en la Plaza de San Juan. Allí hay muchas cosas. Por ejemplo, el cine y la pizzería* 8. **están** *al lado del colegio. También hay un café cerca.*

*Bueno, ¿qué tal las clases este año? ¿Cómo* 9. **están** *Felipe y Marcos? Escríbeme pronto y cuéntame todo.*

*Un abrazo,*
*Franco*

**9** Silvia has never been the neatest person in the world, but this is ridiculous! She can't find anything in her room. Using the drawing of her room, answer her questions using the prepositions in the box.

MODELO la mochila
SILVIA ¿Dónde está mi mochila?
TÚ **Está debajo de la cama.**

| | |
|---|---|
| encima de | debajo de |
| al lado de | cerca de |

1. ¡Ay, pero soy un desastre! ¿Dónde están mis zapatos?
**Un zapato está cerca de la lámpara. Un zapato está debajo de la cama.**

2. Tengo clase. ¿Dónde están mis libros?
**Están al lado de la ropa.**

3. ¡Mi tarea! ¿Dónde está?
**Está debajo del escritorio.**

4. ¡El dinero! ¿Dónde está el dinero?
**Está encima de la computadora.**

5. Llamamos *(Let's call)* a Rafael. ¿Pero dónde está el teléfono?
**Está en el armario. / Está cerca de unos papeles.**

6. Quiero tocar la guitarra. ¿Pero dónde está?
**Está encima de la cama y debajo de la ropa.**

7. ¿Dónde está el diccionario?
**Está encima de la mesa. / Está al lado de la lámpara. / Está debajo de la pizza.**

8. Necesito hacer la tarea de matemáticas. ¿Dónde está la calculadora?
**Está encima de la ropa. / Está cerca de la cama.**

9. Mmmm. ¿Dónde está la pizza?
**Está encima del diccionario. / Está al lado de la cama. / Está cerca de la lámpara.**

Nombre ______________________ Clase ____________ Fecha ____________



**10** You know that you don't use subject pronouns in Spanish as often as in English, but you still need to know what pronoun to use when talking to whom. Look over the **Gramática** section on p. 109 of your textbook, then answer the questions below.

What subject pronoun should you use to talk **to** the following people?

1. tu amiga Maripili

**tú**

2. la profesora Benavides

**usted**

3. tu amigo Rodolfo

**tú**

4. tus amigos españoles, Concha y Manolo

**ustedes; vosotros**

What subject pronoun should you use to talk **about** the following people?

5. el Sr. Durán, director del colegio

**él**

6. tu amigo Bernardo

**él**

7. tus amigas Margarita y Susana

**ellas**

8. tú y tu amigo Sergio

**nosotros**

# TERCER PASO

**11** Carolina and Leonora are talking about everyone's plans for the weekend. Read through their conversation and fill in the blanks with the correct form of **ir**.

CAROLINA Oye, Leonora, ¿adónde **vas** tú el sábado?

LEONORA ¿Yo? Bueno, por la mañana **voy** a la piscina para nadar. Marián **va** conmigo. ¿Quieres ir con nosotras? Vamos allá a las doce.

CAROLINA Yo **voy** al cine con Francisco a las doce, pero si tú y Marián **van** a la piscina más tarde, a las cuatro...

LEONORA Ay, chica, lo siento, pero no puedo (*I'm sorry, but I can't*). Mi famila y yo **vamos** a un concierto de jazz. Marián **va** con nosotros. ¿Quieres ir también?

CAROLINA Bueno, a mí me gusta el jazz. ¿A qué hora **van** ustedes?

LEONORA Nosotros **vamos** a las cuatro y media. Entonces, ven (*come*) a mi casa a las cuatro si quieres ir. ¿Está bien?

CAROLINA Perfecto, hasta luego.

**12** Carlos and his friends are always going one place or another. But Carlos is sick today. Put the following information from his phone messages together to ask and tell where everyone's going and what they're going to do today. Follow the model.

MODELO Marta / gimnasio / 3:30 / jugar al voleibol
**¿Adónde va Marta?**
**Marta va al gimnasio a las tres y media para jugar al voleibol.**

1. Joaquín / parque / 4:00 / caminar con el perro
   ¿**Adónde va Joaquín**?
   **Joaquín va al parque a las cuatro para caminar con el perro.**
2. José y Lalo / casa de Marcos / 5:30 / hacer la tarea
   ¿**Adónde van José y Lalo**?
   **José y Lalo van a la casa de Marcos a las cinco y media para hacer la tarea.**
3. Claudia, Leti y Néstor / cine / 7:00
   ¿**Adónde van Claudia, Leti, y Néstor**?
   **Claudia, Leti y Néstor van al cine a las siete.**
4. Eugenia, Iván y tú / restaurante / tomar un refresco
   ¿**Adónde van ustedes**?
   **Eugenia, Iván y yo vamos (Nosotros vamos) al restaurante para tomar un refresco.**
5. tú / parque / ahora / montar en bicicleta
   ¿**Adónde vas tú**?
   **Voy al parque ahora para montar en bicicleta.**

**13** Which day or days of the week do you associate with the following things or activities? Write the day or days you associate with each, then explain why.

MODELO lavar el carro
**los domingos: En mi casa, siempre lavamos el carro los domingos.**

1. los deportes **Answers will vary.**
2. ir a un restaurante ______________________
3. los bailes ______________________
4. mirar la televisión ______________________
5. lavar la ropa ______________________
6. organizar mi cuarto ______________________
7. ir al centro comercial ______________________
8. descansar ______________________
9. trabajar ______________________

**14** What are your favorite and least favorite days of the week? Explain why you like or don't like each of these days, as in the **modelo**.

MODELO los sábados, los jueves
**Me gustan los sábados porque voy al cine con mis amigos.**
**No me gustan los jueves porque organizo mi cuarto.**

**Answers will vary.**

**15** It's getting close to the holidays and your calendar is filling up fast! To keep track of everything, make an agenda for the coming week. For each day, list one thing you want or need to do, and a place you will go. Use the expressions **necesito** + infinitive, **quiero** + infinitive, and **voy a…** .

MODELO **El lunes necesito estudiar. Voy al cine con Diego.**

| AGENDA PARA LA SEMANA QUE VIENE | |
|---|---|
| **lunes** | Answers will vary. |
| **martes** | |
| **miércoles** | |
| **jueves** | |
| **viernes** | |

**16** Imagine that Esteban, a friend of yours from Mexico, is coming to visit you in a few weeks. He'll come on a Saturday and leave the following Wednesday. Write him a postcard telling him your plans for the two of you. For each day, mention one place the two of you will go, and what you'll do there. Remember to ask Esteban if he likes the activities and places you've included in your plans!

Answers will vary.

Esteban Carrillo Puente
C/ Delicias 18, 3-A
Taxco 31, México

Nombre ______________________ Clase ______________ Fecha ______________



# VAMOS A LEER

**17** To the right is part of a brochure advertising different activities offered at the YMCA sports club in Buenos Aires, Argentina. Look over the page and answer the following questions.

**a.** The ad lists four main topics. Look over what's listed under each of these topics, then match each topic to its English equivalent below.

__c__ 1. deportes
__d__ 2. actividades socio-culturales
__a__ 3. instalaciones
__b__ 4. gimnasia

a. *facilities*
b. *gymnastics*
c. *sports*
d. *social and cultural activities*

## ACJ. A 5 minutos de la oficina.

**GIMNASIA:**
- Mantenimiento.
- Aero-local.
- Step training.
- Low impact.
- Body scultura.
- Cross training.
- Yoga.
- Streching.
- Rehabilitación cardiovascular.
- Aquaerobic.
- Relax time.
- Tai chi chuan.

**ACTIVIDADES SOCIO CULTURALES:**
- Ajedrez.
- Fotografía.
- Tango.
- Folklore.
- Teatro.
- Salidas y excurciones.
- Campamentos.

**DEPORTES:**
- Natación.
- Papi-fútbol.
- Básquetbol.
- Vóleibol.
- Racquet-ball.
- Pelota mano.
- Karate.
- Aerobismo.
- Buceo.

**INSTALACIONES:**
- Piletas climatizadas.
- Gimnasios cerrados.
- Solarium.
- Gimnasio de pesas y complementos.
- Pista aeróbica.
- Baño sauna.
- Canchas de pelota a mano.
- Restaurant y confitería.

**ASOCIACION CRISTIANA DE JOVENES (YMCA)**
Informes planta baja de lunes a viernes de 9 a 20 hs. y sábados de 9 a 12 hs.
Reconquista 439 - 311-4785/86/87 313-8953/8938

**b.** Can you figure out which sports go on in which part of the Buenos Aires YMCA? Match up each **deporte** with its correct **instalación**.

__c__ 1. natación
__d__ 2. pelota a mano
__a__ 3. aerobismo
__b__ 4. basquetbol y voleibol

a. pista aeróbica
b. gimnasios cerrados
c. piletas climatizadas
d. canchas de pelota a mano

**c.** Now look more carefully at the listings under **Gimnasia**, **Deportes**, and **Actividades**. Many of the words are cognates, so you should see words you recognize and understand. Make a list below of at least three sports and activities offered at the Buenos Aires YMCA that you like and three that you don't like.

**Answers will vary.**

Text from advertisement for "Asociación Cristiana de Jóvenes (YMCA)." Reprinted by permission of *Asociación Cristiana de Jóvenes (YMCA)*.

# CULTURA

**18** Decide if the following statements were probably made by **a)** a student in the United States, **b)** a student in a Spanish-speaking country, or **c)** both.

__a__ 1. A las cuatro, voy a la reunión (*meeting*) del Club de drama.

__a__ 2. Este año, quiero participar en el club de computadoras de mi colegio. ¡Me gustan mucho los videojuegos!

__b__ 3. Los domingos, siempre vamos a la casa de mis abuelos o caminamos en el parque.

__c__ 4. Después de clases, por lo general voy a casa para hacer la tarea para mañana.

__a__ 5. Hoy tengo entrenamiento (*practice*) de karate. Mi colegio tiene un equipo de karate excelente.

__b__ 6. Después de clases, a veces tomo un refresco con unos amigos en el café, o caminamos en el parque.

__b__ 7. Esta semana mi equipo de fútbol va a jugar contra el equipo de Taxco. ¡Va a ser un partido padrísimo!

**19** Your class has just received a letter from the **Colegio Reforma** in Cuernavaca, Mexico. They have a lot of questions about life and school in the U.S. You've been assigned to answer the questions given below. Write a short paragraph in Spanish answering the questions below.

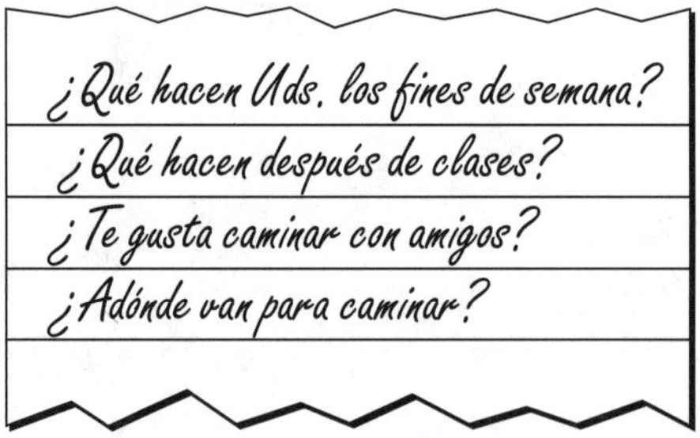
¿Qué hacen Uds. los fines de semana?
¿Qué hacen después de clases?
¿Te gusta caminar con amigos?
¿Adónde van para caminar?

**Answers will vary.**

Nombre ______________________ Clase ______________ Fecha ______________

# El ritmo de la vida

## DE ANTEMANO

**1** Armando is a new student at Seminole High School in Miami. First read the letter he wrote to his cousin Yolanda in Panama about his new home and new routine, then answer the questions below.

**Miami, 8 de noviembre**

**Querida Yolanda,**

**¿Cómo estás? Yo, muy bien. Aquí el ritmo de la vida es increíble. Hay muchísimas cosas que hacer en los ratos libres. Durante la semana, estoy muy ocupado. Los lunes y los jueves tengo la clase de artes marciales. Me gustan mucho el karate y el tae-kwon-do. Los martes tenemos la reunión del Club de arte de mi colegio. ¡Este año quiero ser presidente del club! Los miércoles y los viernes toco la batería en la banda del colegio. Tocamos en los partidos de fútbol todos los viernes por la noche. Los sábados por la noche, a veces vamos a una discoteca para bailar, o a una fiesta en casa de amigos. Los domingos, voy con mamá y papá a comer en un restaurante cubano. Pienso que la comida cubana es fantástica... a mis padres les gusta mucho también.**

**Bueno, escríbeme y cuéntame cómo están todos. Un fuerte abrazo para ti y para mis tíos.**

**Con cariño,**
**Armando**

Look at Armando's schedule. Based on what he wrote in his letter, decide if all of the information is accurate. Check **sí** if it is correct. Check **no** if it is not. For the items that are not correct, fill in the calendar with the correct information.

| | | sí | no |
|---|---|---|---|
| **lunes** | *clase de artes marciales* | ✓ | |
| **martes** | *reunión del Club de español*<br>reunión del Club de arte | | ✓ |
| **miércoles** | *toca la batería con la orquesta*<br>toca la batería con la banda | | ✓ |
| **jueves** | *clase de arte*<br>clase de artes marciales | | ✓ |
| **viernes** | *toca la batería con la banda* | ✓ | |
| **sábado** | *va a la discoteca* | ✓ | |
| **domingo** | *va a un restaurante chino*<br>va a un restaurante cubano | | ✓ |

# PRIMER PASO

**2** Xóchitl hasn't seen her grandmother for a while. Read the questions her **abuela** (*grandmother*) asks her, then write Xóchitl's responses, using the cues in parentheses. Follow the model.

MODELO Mi hija, ¡estás muy delgada! ¿No desayunas? (siempre)
**Sí, abuela, siempre desayuno.**

1. ¡Xóchitl! ¿Nunca organizas tu cuarto? ¡Es un desastre! (a veces)
**Sí, abuela. Organizo mi cuarto a veces.**

2. Xóchitl, ¿todavía tocas el piano? Tócame (*Play me*) algo de Beethoven. (nunca)
**No, abuela, no toco el piano nunca./No, abuela, nunca toco el piano.**

3. Xóchitl, ¿con qué frecuencia ayudas en casa? (todos los días)
**Ayudo en casa todos los días.**

4. Xóchitl, ¿vas al cine con tus amigos durante la semana? (sólo cuando no tengo tarea)
**Sí, abuela, pero sólo cuando no tengo tarea.**



**3** Using the cues provided, write a true statement that each person might make using **siempre** or **no (nunca)**. Base your answers on what you know and on the cultural information you've learned so far.

MODELO **Alma, Lawrence, Kansas:** tener nueve clases al día
**Aquí nunca tenemos nueve clases al día.**

1. **Juan, New York, New York:** regresar a casa a las doce del día para el almuerzo.
**Nunca regreso a casa a las doce para el almuerzo.**

2. **Conchita, Oaxaca, México:** En el colegio, tener por lo menos (*at least*) ocho asignaturas.
**Siempre tengo ocho asignaturas en el colegio.**

3. **Marcos, Valencia, España:** Para ir a la casa de un amigo, tomar el autobús.
**Para ir a la casa de un amigo, siempre tomamos el autobús.**

4. **Lourdes, San Ysidro, California:** En mi colegio, haber clases después de las tres y media de la tarde.
**En mi colegio, nunca hay clases después de las tres y media de la tarde.**

**4** What's it like to be a millionaire at sixteen? Read this interview between **Música y más** magazine and Adrián, a teenage star. Then respond to the statements that follow with **cierto** or **falso**. Correct the false statements.

## **Música y más** entrevista a... *Adrián Sandoval*

**M y m** Seguro, Adrián, que no tienes tiempo para muchas cosas...

**Adrián** Bueno, ¡soy más normal de lo que piensas! (*I'm more normal than you think!*) Siempre tengo tiempo para mis amigos.

**M y m** Tienes una vida social muy ocupada (*a very busy social life*), ¿verdad?

**Adrián** A veces necesito cantar en conciertos o en programas de televisión. Pero, generalmente (*usually*), durante la semana estoy en casa.

**M y m** ¿Y cómo es un día típico?

**Adrián** Bueno, siempre desayuno. Después voy al colegio.

**M y m** ¡Qué bien! Y después del colegio, ¿qué haces?

**Adrián** A ver, a veces necesito trabajar en el estudio. Y necesito hacer la tarea todos los días.

**M y m** ¿Y los fines de semana?

**Adrián** Bueno, muchas veces no hago nada. Pero a veces me gusta ir con amigos a un restaurante o al cine, pero sólo cuando no tengo mucha tarea.

**M y m** Ya eres millonario, ¿no? ¿Y todavía ayudas en casa?

**Adrián** ¡Siempre! Muchas veces cuido a mis hermanos, y a veces aun (*even*) preparo la comida.

**M y m** ¿Y qué tal la comida que preparas?

**Adrián** ¡Horrible! ¡Guácala! (*Yuck!*)

1. Adrián no necesita cantar en conciertos todos los días.
   **Cierto.**

2. Muchas veces Adrián no desayuna porque está atrasado.
   **Falso. Adrián desayuna todos los días.**

3. Adrián siempre hace muchas cosas los fines de semana.
   **Falso. A veces no hace nada.**

4. Durante la semana va con amigos a un restaurante o al cine.
   **Falso. Durante la semana está en casa.**

5. Adrián siempre prepara la comida.
   **Falso. A veces prepara la comida.**

**5** Make a list in Spanish of four things you never do, and explain why you never do them. Look at the vocabulary list for Chapter 5 if you need some ideas.

MODELO Nunca voy a los partidos de fútbol del colegio porque siempre trabajo los sábados por la mañana en el supermercado.

**Answers will vary.**

**6** Who are your favorite people? Answer the questions below, explaining why each person or group of people is your favorite.

MODELO ¿Quién es tu persona favorita?
**Mi "persona" favorita es mi perro Sam. No es una persona, pero es muy simpático y cómico.**

1. ¿Quién es tu profesor/a favorito/a? **Answers will vary.**
2. ¿Quién es tu cantante (*singer*) favorito? ______________________
3. ¿Quién es tu mejor amigo o amiga? ______________________
4. ¿Quiénes son tus atletas favoritos? ______________________

**7** What kind of life do you lead? Is it too busy, too disorganized, or just right? Take the following magazine poll to analyze your lifestyle. Answer each question based on what's true for you. Keep track of how many **a.**, **b.** and **c.** answers you've circled, and then read the article's description of your personality and lifestyle. Is it correct?

## ¿Te gusta el ritmo de tu vida?

**1.** ¿Con qué frecuencia haces la tarea?
**a.** siempre
**b.** a veces
**c.** nunca

**2.** ¿Con qué frecuencia descansas o tomas la siesta (*do you take a nap*)?
**a.** nunca o casi nunca
**b.** a veces
**c.** todos los días

**3.** ¿Con qué frecuencia organizas tu cuarto?
**a.** todos los días
**b.** sólo cuando sea (*it's*) necesario
**c.** nunca

**4.** ¿Con qué frecuencia vas al cine con tus amigos?
**a.** nunca
**b.** a veces
**c.** todos los días

**5.** ¿Con qué frecuencia lavas los platos?
**a.** todos los días
**b.** a veces
**c.** nunca

**6.** ¿Con qué frecuencia miras la televisión?
**a.** nunca
**b.** sólo a veces, para mirar mis programas favoritos
**c.** siempre

**7.** ¿Con qué frecuencia sacas la basura?
**a.** siempre
**b.** a veces
**c.** nunca

**8.** ¿Con qué frecuencia practicas un deporte?
**a.** nunca
**b.** a veces
**c.** todos los días

### Análisis:

**a.**—Si la mayoría (*most*) de tus respuestas son **a.**, entonces trabajas mucho—¡y es un problema! Tienes un ritmo de vida muy complicado. Necesitas descansar más y hacer cosas divertidas en tu tiempo libre.

**b.**—Si la mayoría de tus respuestas son **b.**, está bien. Eres una persona equilibrada. En tu vida hay un balance entre las responsabilidades y el tiempo libre. Trabajas, pero también descansas.

**c.**—Si la mayoría de tus respuestas son **c.**, entonces descansas mucho—¡y es un problema! Tienes un ritmo de vida desorganizado. Necesitas ser más responsable y organizado en tus estudios.

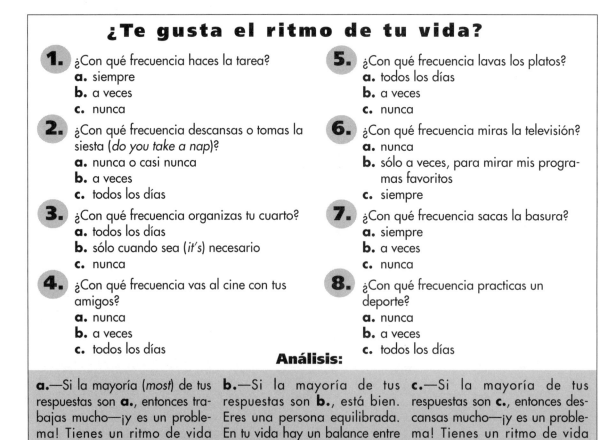

Nombre ____________ Clase ____________ Fecha ____________

# SEGUNDO PASO

**8** Next year you will be an exchange student in Montevideo. Below is a letter from Clara, your host student, about what she and her friends like to do in their spare time. Read Clara's letter and complete it with the correct words or phrases from the box.

**les nos te a ellos le me a ellas**

*Querido amigo,*

*¡Hola! Me llamo Clara Serrano, y soy de Montevideo, Uruguay. A mí* 1. **me** *gustan muchas cosas: montar en bicicleta en el parque, comer pizza en el centro y pasar el rato con mis amigos. Después de clases, a nosotros* 2. **nos** *gusta ir al cine. A mi amigo Leonardo* 3. **le** *gustan las películas de aventuras. Mis amigas Carmen y Rebeca son simpáticas.* 4. **A ellas** *les gustan las películas de ciencia ficción. Y qué curiosos son mis amigos Horacio y Abel.* 5. **A ellos** *les gustan mucho las películas de horror. Vamos al cine dos veces por semana. A mí* 6. **me** *gusta ir por la tarde, pero a mis amigos* 7. **les** *gusta ir por la noche. ¿A ti* 8. **te** *gusta ir al cine? ¿Qué películas* 9. **te** *gustan?*

**9** For each of the drawings below, write a sentence explaining what the people pictured like, or don't like, to do. Then say how often they do the activities shown.

**Marta y Susana**

**Isabel y Bingo**

**Joaquín y Laura**

**David y Micaela**

1. **Answers will vary. Possible Answers: A Marta y a Susana no les gusta organizar su cuarto. No organizan su cuarto nunca.**
2. **A Isabel y a Bingo les gusta caminar en el parque. Isabel camina con Bingo todos los días.**
3. **A Joaquín y a Laura les gusta jugar al tenis. Juegan al tenis el martes y el sábado.**
4. **A David y a Micaela no les gusta jugar al voleibol en la clase de educación física. Tienen la clase los lunes y los miércoles.**

Nombre ______________________ Clase ____________ Fecha ____________



**10** Imagine that you have a twin brother named Silvio. You both like to do many of the same things. Look at the lists of favorite activities for you and your twin. If only one of you likes an activity, write a sentence saying which one of you likes it. If you both like an activity, write a sentence saying that you like to do that activity together.

| Yo | Silvio |
|---|---|
| esquiar | pescar |
| acampar | acampar |
| bucear | hacer ejercicio |
| correr por la playa | correr por la playa |
| hacer ejercicio | bucear |

**Answers will vary. Possible Answers:**

1. **A mí me gusta esquiar.**
2. **A Silvio le gusta pescar.**
3. **A nosotros nos gusta acampar juntos.**
4. **Nos gusta bucear juntos.**
5. **Nos gusta hacer ejercicio juntos.**
6. **Nos gusta correr por la playa juntos.**

**11** The sentences below describe what some students and teachers at Seminole High School do in their free time. Complete the sentences with the correct forms of the verbs in parentheses, then check your answers by filling in the crossword puzzle with the missing words.

**Horizontales**

2. En la clase de literatura, nosotros ____ muchas novelas. (leer)
5. Todos los estudiantes ____ la reunión a las tres y media. (asistir a)
7. Martín y yo ____ un concierto este sábado. (asistir a)
9. Yo ____ una carta a mi amigo en La Habana todos los martes. (escribir)
10. Yo siempre ____ un sándwich en el almuerzo. (comer)
12. Santiago y Teresa ____ cartas cuando tienen tiempo. (escribir)
13. Nosotros ____ tacos en la cafetería del colegio los miércoles. (comer)

**Verticales**

1. Fátima y yo ____ una carta de España todos los sábados. (recibir)
2. Por la mañana, yo ____ el periódico en casa (leer).
3. Ricardo, ¿cuándo ____ la tarea, por la tarde o por la noche? (hacer)
4. ¿Qué ____ Elena después de clases? (hacer)
6. En la clase de historia, nosotros ____ composiciones. (escribir)
8. Nosotros siempre ____ agua después de correr. (beber)
10. El Sr. Guzmán y su perro Bobby ____ en el parque los fines de semana. (correr)
11. Germán y Lola ____ sus libros de texto en el autobús. (leer)

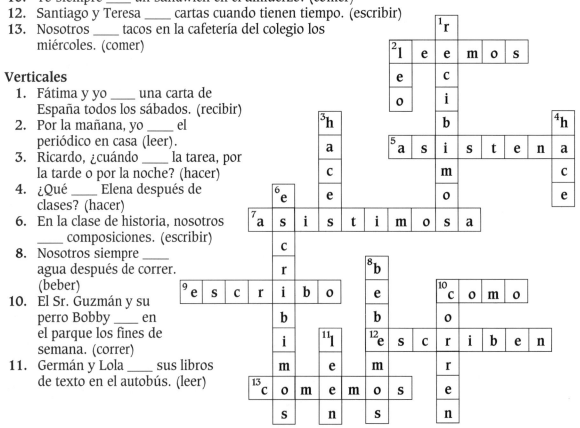

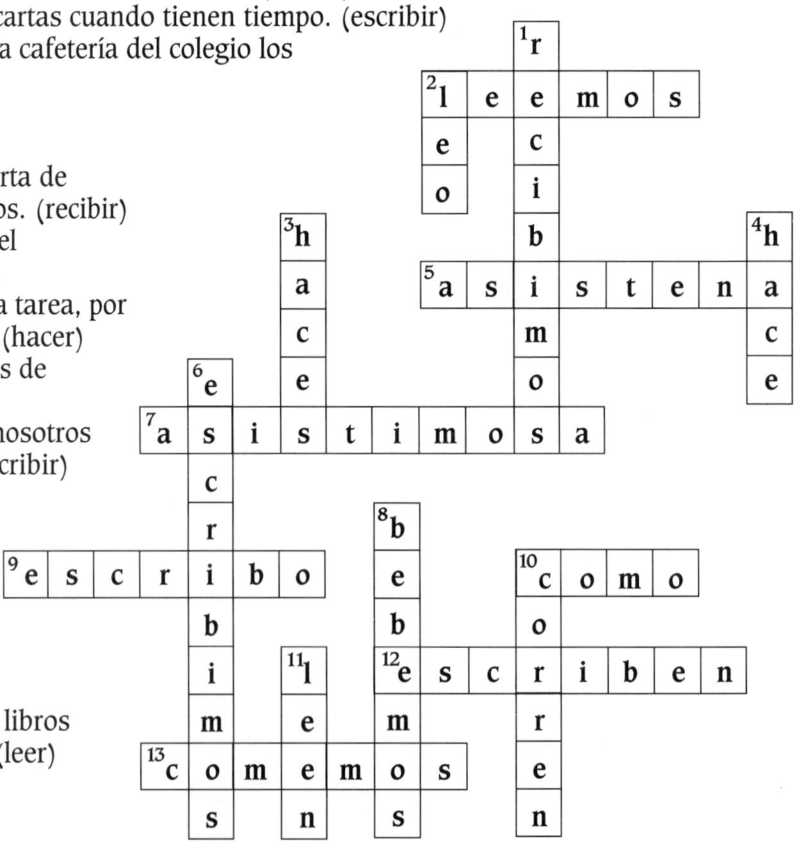

Nombre ____________________ Clase ____________ Fecha ____________

**12** The planet Xargon has sent a team of investigators to find out about our planet and its inhabitants. You have been chosen to interpret the Xargonians' interviews for a Spanish-speaking audience. First write out the Xargonians' questions (items 1, 3, and 5). Then write what the earthlings answered, using expressions from the box below.

**todos los días** **sólo cuando...** **muchas veces** **durante...** **a veces** **por la mañana** **siempre** **por la noche** **nunca** **por la tarde**

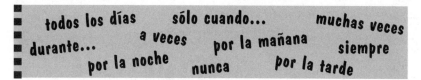

1. (The Xargonians want to know how often earthlings go to school.)
**Answers will vary. Some possible answers: ¿Con qué frecuencia van al colegio? ¿Van al colegio...?**

2. **Voy al colegio todos los días, de lunes a viernes. Voy por la mañana y por la tarde.**

3. (The Xargonians want to know what students do after class.)
**¿Qué hacen los estudiantes después de clase?**

4. **Después de clase, muchas veces vamos al centro comercial o a la pizzería. A veces vamos al cine, o regresamos a casa.**

5. (The Xargonians want to know if students like to talk on the phone and how often.)
**¿A tus amigos y a ti les gusta hablar por teléfono? ¿Con qué frecuencia?**

6. **Sí, nos gusta hablar por teléfono. Hablamos sólo cuando no tenemos mucha tarea.**

# TERCER PASO

**13** By now you've learned how to talk about what day, month, and season it is in Spanish. Unscramble the words whose definitions appear below. If you unscramble each word correctly, you will find a question in the shaded vertical column.

MODELO **m a r z o** (r m a o z) (El mes después de febrero)

1. **m i é r c o l e s** (e l m c é i o r s) El día entre (*between*) el martes y el jueves.
2. **o c t u b r e** (c r b e u o t) El mes antes de noviembre.
3. **s á b a d o** (b s d á a o) El día después del viernes.
4. **a b r i l** (i l b r a) El mes entre marzo y mayo.
5. **v e r a n o** (a v r o n e) La estación antes del otoño.
6. **m a r t e s** (s m e t r a) El día después del lunes.
7. **l u n e s** (e l n s u) El día después del domingo.
8. **p r i m a v e r a** (e r p a v i m a r) La estación antes del verano.
9. **f e c h a** (h a f c e) La palabra en español para *date*.
10. **i n v i e r n o** (v o n r i i e n) La estación antes de la primavera.
11. **d i c i e m b r e** (e r d m c b e i i) El mes después de noviembre.
12. **h o y** (y h o) El día antes de mañana.
13. **a g o s t o** (t a o g o s) El mes entre julio y septiembre.

**14** Your pen pal Rosario from Perú wants to know about some U.S. holidays. Tell Rosario the date of the following special days this year.

1. El Día de la Independencia **El Día de la Independencia es el 4 de julio.**
2. El Día de Acción de Gracias (*Thanksgiving*) **El Día de Acción de Gracias es el ... de noviembre.**
3. El primer día del verano **El primer día del verano es el 21 de junio.**
4. El Día de San Valentín **El Día de San Valentín es el 14 de febrero.**
5. El Año Nuevo **El Año Nuevo es el primero de enero.**
6. Tu cumpleaños (*birthday*) **Mi cumpleaños es el...**

**15** It's easy to forget which season some months fall in! Read Javier's and Miguel's conversation, filling in the blanks with the correct seasons and months.

JAVIER Oye, Miguel, ¿cuál es tu estación favorita? La primavera, ¿verdad?

MIGUEL ¡Ya sabes que me gusta más el verano! Los meses de **junio**, **julio** y **agosto**, cuando hace calor y voy a la piscina a nadar todos los días.

JAVIER Y el mes de septiembre, también, ¿no?

MIGUEL No, hombre. Septiembre es un mes de **otoño**.

JAVIER Ah, sí, tienes razón *(you're right)*. Con **octubre** y **noviembre**.

MIGUEL Y no te olvides de *(don't forget about)* diciembre.

JAVIER No, diciembre está en **el invierno**. También los meses de **enero** y **febrero**.

MIGUEL Y, por fin, **marzo**, **abril** y **mayo** son meses de **la primavera**.

**16** For each of the illustrations below, write what season it is and what the weather is usually like where you live.

1.  octubre **Answers will vary. Possible answers: Es el otoño. Hace fresco.**

2.  junio **Es el verano. Hace sol.**

3.  abril **Es la primavera. Está lloviendo./Llueve./Está nublado.**

4. 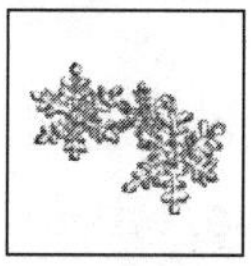 enero **Es el invierno. Está nevando./Nieva./Está nublado.**

5. 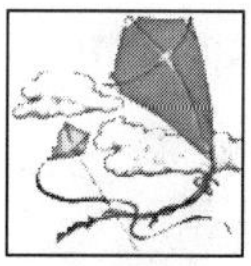 marzo **Es la primavera. Hace mucho viento.**

6.  julio **Es el verano. Hace mucho calor.**

**17** The weather can have a big effect on our daily activities. Look at the drawings of people below, and write one or two sentences describing what the people shown are doing or where they're going, and what the weather is like.

1. Elena y Sergio

2. El Sr. Jiménez

3. Susanita y Benjamín

4. Doña Blanca

1. **Elena y Sergio están en casa porque está lloviendo. Miran la televisión y comen sándwiches.**
2. **El Sr. Jiménez corre por la playa porque hace buen tiempo. No hace mucho viento. Hace fresco.**
3. **Susanita y Benjamín van al parque para jugar porque hace viento.**
4. **Doña Blanca lee una novela y escucha música en casa porque está nevando y hace frío.**



**18** What's your favorite time of year? Write a short paragraph of about eight sentences in which you tell what season you like best and why. What's the weather like? What kinds of things do you and your friends like to do then?

**Answers will vary. Possible Answers: Me gusta el verano porque tengo vacaciones. En el verano hace calor y no llueve mucho. Todos los días hace buen tiempo. Mis amigos y yo nadamos y buceamos. También jugamos al voleibol en la playa y acampamos. Los fines de semana vamos al centro comercial porque nos gusta jugar videojuegos. Muchas veces nosotros vamos al cine y luego tomamos un helado.**

Nombre ______________________ Clase ____________ Fecha ____________

# VAMOS A LEER

**19** Read the two comic strips, then answer the questions below.

**me molesta** = *bothers me* **humedad** = *humidity* **salta** = *jump out*

**tontas** = *stupid* **asoleado** = *sunny* **regadera** = *watering can*
**influir sobre sus mentes** = *to play with their minds*

**a.** Check your comprehension by answering the following questions.

1. Why isn't Hobbes (the tiger) going to like the end of his wagon ride? **Possible answer: He is going to land in the water.**

2. How do you think Hobbes would describe Calvin in the last frame of the second strip? Write a caption in Spanish to express what he thinks of Calvin.
**Possible answer: ¡Qué malo! Él no es nada divertido.**

**b.** Read the following descriptions of Calvin and Hobbes and decide if they are accurate. If so, circle **sí**. If not, circle **no**. Then correct all of the information that is not accurate.

1. Calvin es alto, moreno y antipático. sí (no) **1. bajo, rubio, travieso**
2. A Calvin no le gusta jugar. sí (no) **2. le gusta jugar**
3. Hobbes es cómico, inteligente y simpático. (sí) no
4. A Calvin y Hobbes les gusta pasar el rato juntos. (sí) no

Nombre ______________________ Clase ____________ Fecha ____________

# CULTURA

**20** Based upon what you've learned about Spanish-speaking young people, correct the following statements if they are false.

1. It's fairly common for young people in Spain or Latin America to have their own cars.
   **Falso. Young Spanish-speakers are more likely to take public transportation or walk.**

2. Spanish-speaking young people often will make plans to meet friends in a park, a café or some other public place.
   **Cierto**

3. The streets of the average town or city in a Spanish-speaking country will most likely be deserted after sundown.
   **Falso. People often go out at night and stay up rather late.**

4. Young people in the Spanish-speaking world often tend to socialize in groups.
   **Cierto**

**21** Imagine that you're a travel agent, specializing in trips to Latin America. What kind of clothing would you advise your customers to take with them if they're going to . . .? Explain briefly what the weather is like in each case.

1. make a trip to Argentina in December and January
   **Answers will vary. Possible answers: summer clothes/ warm → hot weather**

2. travel to southern Chile in mid-July
   **winter clothes**

3. take a tour of the Andean region of Ecuador in May
   **warm clothes**

**22** Imagine that you're going to spend the month of January in Buenos Aires, Argentina. Through an exchange program, you'll be living with an Argentine family with two kids your age. In this chapter you've read about Spanish-speaking young people and about the climate in southern South America. Based on what you've learned in this chapter, what might you expect to see and experience with your host family in Buenos Aires?

**Answers will vary.**

Nombre ________________ Clase ____________ Fecha ____________

# Entre familia

## DE ANTEMANO

**1** When Raquel shows Armando her family's photo album, he asks some questions about her family. Can you match Armando's questions with Raquel's answers?

b 1. ¿De dónde es tu tía Luisa?

e 2. ¿Dónde vive tu hermano Carlos ahora?

d 3. A ustedes les gusta la música, ¿verdad?

a 4. ¿Qué hacen ustedes durante las vacaciones de Navidad?

c 5. ¿Sales mucho con tus hermanos?

a. Para Navidades, vamos a Tampa y visitamos a mis tíos y mis abuelos que viven allí.

b. Ella es de Cuba, como mis padres.

c. Sí, salgo con ellos bastante. Muchas veces voy con mis hermanos al cine o al centro comercial. ¡A veces salimos a escuchar música!

d. ¡Muchísimo! Todos tocamos por lo menos un instrumento musical.

e. Ahora él vive en Gainesville. Estudia en la Universidad de Florida.

**2** Look at the family portraits and circle the description that best matches each portrait.

1.

a. Ésta es mi familia: mis padres, mi hermano, mi hermana y mi abuela.
(b.) Aquí estamos todos: mi madre, mi padre, mi hermano y yo.
c. Aquí ves a mi familia: mi padre, mi madre, mi hermana, nuestro perro y yo.

2.

a. Éstos son mis hermanos.
b. En esta foto estamos todos: mi padre, mi madre y yo.
(c.) Éstos son mis abuelos.

3.

a. Éstos son mis padres.
(b.) Ésta es mi familia: mis padres, mis dos hermanos menores y yo.
c. Ésta es mi familia: mis padres, mis dos primos y mi abuelo.

Nombre ______________________ Clase ____________ Fecha ____________

# PRIMER PASO

**3** Look over the **Vocabulario** on p. 153 of your textbook, then complete the crossword puzzle.

**Horizontales**

5. El padre de tu padre
8. El hijo de tu madre y tu padrastro
10. Lo contrario de (*The opposite of*) hermano
12. La hermana de tu padre
13. Los hijos de tu tío
14. La madre de tu padre
15. Las hijas de tus tíos

**Verticales**

1. El hermano de tu madre
2. Lo contrario de padre
3. La hija de tu madrastra o tu padrastro
4. Lo contrario de esposa
6. El hijo de tu abuelo y el esposo de tu madre
7. El esposo de tu madre, pero que no es tu verdadero (*real*) padre
9. La esposa de tu padre, pero que no es tu verdadera madre
10. Tu padre es el ___ de tu abuela paterna
11. Tu madre es la ___ de tu abuelo materno

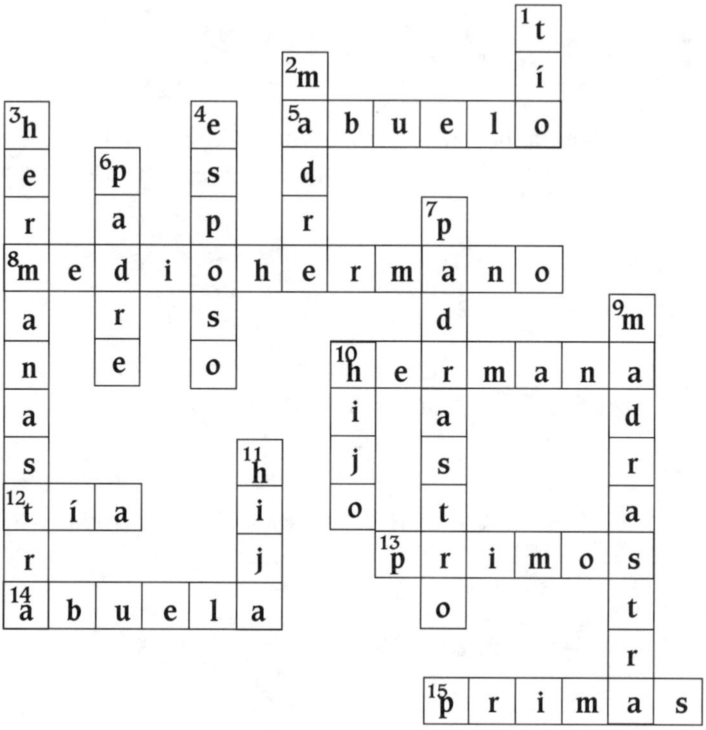


**4** Guillermo Montes has invited Lupe to his house for a family party. She's never met any of his family before. As his relatives come into the living room, Guillermo points out everyone to Lupe. Complete his sentences with **éste**, **ésta**, **éstos**, or **éstas**.

1. ___Éstas___ son mis primas, Rosita y Carmen. Son estudiantes en la Universidad de Florida. Y 2. ___ésta___ es mi abuelita. Ella vive con nosotros. 3. ___Éstos___ son mis hermanitos, Alfonso y Carlitos. Son super-pesados (*pains*). 4. ___Ésta___ es mi madre. A ella le gustan mucho las fiestas grandes. 5. ___Éstos___ son mis tíos, Isabel y Armando. Ellos viven en Orlando. 6. ___Ésta___ es mi hermana mayor, Gloria... ¡ y 7. ___éste___ es mi sobrinito, Javier! Sólo tiene seis meses, pero ya sé que es muy inteligente. Y 8. ___éste___ es mi padre. A él le gustan las fiestas, pero prefiere (*he prefers*) leer el periódico.

**5** Imagine that you're having a conversation with Pilar Guzmán Franco about her family. Using her family tree and the cues provided, write your questions and Pilar's answers.

1. TÚ (Ask how many people there are in Pilar's family.)
   **¿Cuántas personas hay en tu familia?**
2. PILAR **Hay once personas en mi familia./Somos once.**
3. TÚ (Ask what Pilar's parents are like.)
   **¿Cómo son tus padres?**
4. PILAR **Possible answers: Mi padre es alto y tiene cincuenta años. Mi madre es estricta pero simpática.**
5. TÚ (Ask what Pilar's grandparents' names are.)
   **¿Cómo se llaman tus abuelos?**
6. PILAR **Mi abuela se llama María y mi abuelo se llama Francisco.**
7. TÚ (Ask if Pilar and her brother have any pets [**animales domésticos**].)
   **¿Tienen ustedes animales domésticos?**
8. PILAR **Sí, tenemos un pez que se llama Tiburón y un perro que se llama Simba.**

**6** The words **su** and **sus** can be confusing, because they mean so many different things: *your, his, her, their*. In a conversation, though, context will make the meaning of these words clear. How many meanings can the expressions below have? Circle all of the English expressions that match each Spanish one. Some expressions may have more than one match.

MODELO su hijo
**a.** el hijo de él **b.** los hijos de ella **c.** el hijo de ustedes

1. su casa
   **a.** la casa de ella **b.** la casa de ustedes **c.** las casas de usted
2. sus abuelos
   **a.** la abuela de ellos **b.** los abuelos de usted **c.** los abuelos de ustedes
3. su hermano
   **a.** el hermano de él **b.** los hermanos de ellos **c.** el hermano de ustedes
4. su madrastra
   **a.** la madrastra de nosotros **b.** la madrastra de María **c.** la madrastra de ustedes
5. sus padres
   **a.** los padres de ustedes **b.** el padre de ellas **c.** los padres de nosotras
6. su familia
   **a.** la familia de Pedro y Juan **b.** la familia de ustedes **c.** la familia de usted
7. sus primos
   **a.** los primos de nosotros **b.** el primo de ellas **c.** los primos de Lupe
8. sus tíos
   **a.** los tíos de Pilar **b.** los tíos de ella **c.** los tíos de ustedes

**7** Complete Carmen's description of her family with the corrrect possessive adjectives.

¡Hola! Me llamo Carmen Iriarte y soy de Nueva York. Te quiero describir a **1.** ___**mi**___ *(my)* familia. 2. ___**Nuestra**___ *(Our)* familia es un poco complicada—somos muy internacionales. 3. ___**Mi**___ *(My)* madre se llama Ana y es de Argentina originalmente. Ahora vive aquí en Nueva York. **4.** ___**Su**___ *(Her)* hermano Roberto vive aquí también. **5.** ___**Su**___ *(His)* esposa es de Irlanda. Se llama Maureen. **6.** ___**Sus**___ *(Their)* dos hijitos se llaman Brian y Sara. Me encanta ir a la casa de **7.** ___**mis**___ *(my)* tíos Roberto y Maureen y jugar con **8.** ___**mis**___ *(my)* dos sobrinitos. **9.** ___**Sus**___ *(their)* videojuegos son super-divertidos.

**10.** ___**Mis**___ *(My)* padres están divorciados. **11.** ___**Mi**___ *(My)* padre Antonio es español. Vive ahora en España con **12.** ___**su**___ *(his)* segunda esposa, Marián. **13.** ___**Su**___ *(their)* casa está en Sevilla. Marián es muy cariñosa. **14.** ___**Su**___ *(Her)* hijo Alfonso es **15.** ___**mi**___ *(my)* hermanastro. Somos muy buenos amigos. Él quiere aprender inglés. Entonces, el año que viene, Alfonso va a vivir en **16.** ___**nuestro**___ *(our)* apartamento en Nueva York y estudiar aquí. ¡Y yo voy a Sevilla a vivir en **17.** ___**su**___ *(his)* piso y estudiar en **18.** ___**su**___ *(his)* colegio. Qué complicado, ¿verdad?

**8** Juan and Daniela Barrón are brother and sister. The pictures below are of their family. Take the role of either Juan or Daniela. First think of a name for each member of the family, and label him or her accordingly (Juan and Daniela are already labeled for you.) Also say how he or she is related to you. Then write a short paragraph answering the following questions.

¿Cuántas personas hay en tu familia? ¿Cómo es tu familia? ¿Cuántas personas viven en tu casa? ¿Tienen un animal doméstico? ¿Quiénes son las personas en estas fotos?

**Answers will vary.**

______________________________________________

______________________________________________

______________________________________________

______________________________________________

# SEGUNDO PASO

**9** Look at the Guzmán family tree in Activity 5. Answer the following questions about members of Pilar's family, using what you've learned in Chapter 6 as well as any other words you know. Use your imagination to describe them.

1. ¿Cómo es Humberto?¿De qué color es su pelo? ¿De qué color son sus ojos? ¿Cuántos años tiene?

   **Answers will vary. Possible answers: Humberto es muy listo. Tiene el pelo negro y los ojos de color café. Él tiene dieciséis años.**

2. ¿Cómo es María? ¿De qué color es su pelo? ¿Cuántos años tiene?

   **María es muy simpática. Tiene canas. Tiene setenta años, pero se ve joven.**

3. ¿Cómo es la madre de Pilar? ¿De qué color es su pelo? ¿Cuántos años tiene?

   **Elena es muy cariñosa. Es pelirroja. Tiene cuarenta y siete años.**

4. ¿Cómo es Simba? ¿De qué color es su pelo?

   **Simba es un poco travieso y muy cómico. Su pelo es de color café.**

**10** How would you describe your best friend? Think of someone you're close to, either a family member or a friend, and write five to six sentences describing that person. Use the adjectives on pp. 158 and 159 of your textbook, as well as any others you've learned. Below are some other words you can use. Many of them are cognates.

| | | |
|---|---|---|
| **comprensivo(a)** *understanding* | **chismoso(a)** *gossipy* | **tener...años** |
| **honrado(a)** *honest* | **(im)paciente** *(im)patient* | **vivir en...** |
| **(in)maduro(a)** *(im)mature* | **irresponsable** *irresponsible* | **le gusta...** |
| **sincero(a)** *sincere* | **valiente** *brave* | |

**Answers will vary.**

Nombre ______________________ Clase ____________ Fecha ____________

**11** Combine elements from the columns to write four original sentences telling how often these people do the activities listed. Use the "personal **a**" as appropriate.

MODELO **Mis padres no visitan a sus primos nunca.**

| | | | |
|---|---|---|---|
| yo | llamar (a) | mis abuelos | nunca |
| mis padres | visitar (a) | un museo | siempre |
| el/la profesor(a) | querer conocer (a) | sus primos | con frecuencia |

1. **Answers will vary.**
2. ______________________
3. ______________________
4. ______________________

**12** Look over this page from Andrés Benavente's address book. Then, using the cues provided, ask him for some information about his family.

1. what his family is like
**¿Cómo es tu familia?**
2. what he and his family do together on weekends
**¿Qué hacen ustedes los fines de semana?**
3. where the people in his family live
**¿Dónde viven tus parientes?**

Now write Andrés's answers to your questions. Mention at least two things in item 5. In item 6, write where Andrés would say at least four members of his family live, including himself. Use your imagination!

4. **Answers will vary. Mi familia es grande y divertida.**
5. **Los fines de semana nosotros visitamos a mis abuelos y vamos al museo.**
6. **Mi abuela vive en Puerto Rico. Mi hermana vive en Florida.**

Jacobo Benavente Dávila
C.P. #278
Arecibo 00613
PUERTO RICO

Ana María Benavente
P.O. Box 8733
University of Florida
Gainesville, FL 31559
(en Miami: 3225 Buena Vista Avenue
Miami, FL 35921)

Benigno Benavente Rubio y
Alma Ybarra de Benavente
C/ Palomar 92, 3
San Juan 00231
PUERTO RICO

Martín Berenger
Carrer dels Angels, 47, 6A
Barcelona 54022
ESPAÑA

Lidia Calero
11 Cra. 5 #6-64 B
Cartagena
COLOMBIA

Alejandro Galdós Sobejano
C/ Arteaga 1483
Colonia Centro, Nuevo Laredo
Tamaulipas MEXICO

Carolina Irizarri de la Vega
C/ 15 de septiembre, 42
Metapán, Sta. Ana
EL SALVADOR

Néstor Muñoz Arévalo
Avda. 13, #59, 7B
Maracaibo VENEZUELA

Nombre ______________________ Clase ____________ Fecha ____________

**13** Mercedes and Laura are tennis partners and friends. Below are their calendars for the next week. Read them and then answer the questions below. Do Mercedes and Laura have anything in common besides tennis?

MODELO ¿Cuándo sale Mercedes con su tía Julia? ¿Qué hacen?
**Mercedes sale con su tía Julia el viernes a la una. Van al centro comercial.**

**EL HORARIO DE MERCEDES**

| lunes 16 | martes 17 | miércoles 18 | jueves 19 | viernes 20 | sábado 21 | domingo 22 |
|---|---|---|---|---|---|---|
| Laura— tenis 4:00 | Mamá— visitar al tío Rubén 3:30 | Miguel— 5:00 biblioteca para el examen de historia | Laura— tenis 4:00 | Tía Julia— 1:00, al centro comercial<br>Mamá y papá— cumpleaños de Abuelo | Roberto— cine 4:30 | Abuela— misa 10:30 |

**EL HORARIO DE LAURA**

| llunes 16 | martes 17 | miércoles 18 | jueves 19 | viernes 20 | sábado 21 | domingo 22 |
|---|---|---|---|---|---|---|
| Mercedes— tenis 4:00 | Sara— Café Gijón, 3:30 | Mamá— regalo para Papá, 3:30 | Mercedes— tenis 4:00 | Roberto— Restaurante La Góndola 8:00 | Mamá y Papá— | ¡PLAYA! |

1. ¿Qué hacen Laura y Mercedes los lunes y los jueves?
**Las dos chicas juegan al tenis a las 4:00 los lunes y los jueves.**

2. ¿Con quién sale Mercedes el miércoles? ¿Adónde van y qué hacen?
**Ella sale con Miguel. Van a la biblioteca y estudian.**

3. ¿Con quién sale Laura el martes? ¿Qué hacen las dos chicas?
**El martes Laura sale con su amiga Sara. Van al Café Gijón y toman un refresco.**

4. ¿Cuándo sale Mercedes con su mamá? ¿Y cuándo sale Laura con su mamá?
**Sale con su mamá el martes. Laura sale con su mamá el miércoles.**

5. ¿Qué hace Mercedes el viernes por la noche, y con quién sale?
**Ella va a la fiesta de cumpleaños de su abuelo el viernes. Sale con sus padres.**

6. ¿Qué hace Laura este fin de semana?
**Este fin de semana Laura va a la playa con sus padres.**

7. ¿Cuándo sale Mercedes con su abuela? ¿Qué hacen?
**Ella sale con su abuela el domingo. Van a misa a las 10:30.**

8. ¿Con quién sale Laura el viernes? ¿Y con quién sale Mercedes el sábado?
**Laura sale con Roberto el viernes a las 8:00. Mercedes sale con Roberto el sábado a las 4:30.**

Nombre ______________________ Clase ____________ Fecha ____________

# TERCER PASO

**14** Match each of the problems pictured below with the most logical solution. Can you think of another solution to each problem?

1. h

2. d

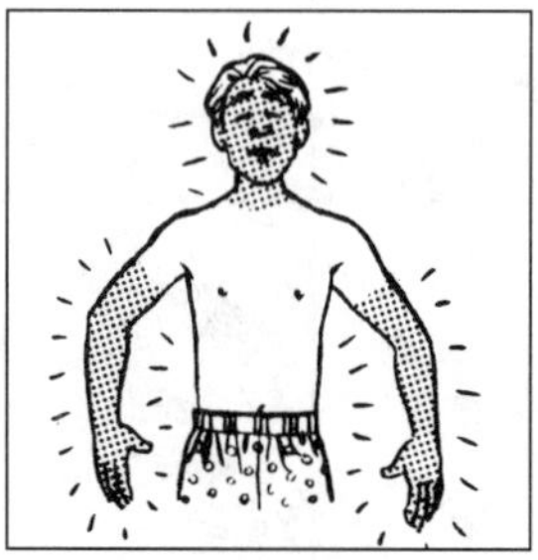

3. f

4. g

5. a

6. b

7. e

8. c

**Soluciones**

**a.** Debes comprar una bicicleta nueva.
**b.** Debes estudiar mucho antes de los exámenes finales.
**c.** Debes dormir *(sleep)* ahora y hacer la tarea mañana.
**d.** No debes ir al cine si no tienes dinero.
**e.** Debes caminar con el perrito por la mañana, por la tarde y por la noche.
**f.** No debes tomar mucho sol en la playa.
**g.** Debes ir al restaurante a comer algo.
**h.** Debes organizar tu cuarto.

**15** For each person listed below, write two sentences: one stating a problem that person or group has, and another stating what the person should do or should not do. Explain your solutions to the problems as in the **modelo**.

MODELO Nuestro colegio...
**Nuestro colegio debe comprar un televisor para la cafetería porque me gusta ver televisión cuando como.**

1. El profesor/La profesora de español... **debe...** ______________________

______________________

2. Mis amigos... **deben...** ______________________

______________________

3. Yo... **debo...** ______________________

______________________

4. Mis padres... **deben...**

5. Mi hermano/a... **debe...**

6. La clase de español... **debe...**

7. El director/La directora del colegio... **debe...**

**16** On weekends, Irene and Merche like to get together and enjoy their free time. But sometimes it's hard to find free time, even on a Saturday morning. Follow the directions to create a phone conversation between Irene and Merche. **Answers will vary. Possible answers are:**

| Irene | Merche |
|---|---|
| Calls up Merche and asks what she is doing. **Hola, ¿qué tal? ¿Qué haces?** | Says that she's cleaning her room now. **Ahora organizo mi cuarto. Es un desastre.** |
| Asks if she wants to go to the mall this afternoon. **¿Quieres ir al centro comercial esta tarde?** | Says yes, but that she must do some things at home first. **Sí, pero debo hacer unas cosas en casa primero.** |
| Asks what she needs to do. **¿Qué debes hacer?** | Mentions three chores she has to do. **Debo pasar la aspiradora, lavar los platos y trabajar en el jardín.** |
| Says that she'll go to her house at 3:00 P.M. **Voy a tu casa a las tres de la tarde.** | Says it's OK, but she needs to cut the grass. **Está bien, pero necesito cortar el césped.** |
| Asks at what time Merche wants to go out. **¿A qué hora quieres salir?** | Says she wants to go at 4:30 P.M. **Quiero ir a las cuatro y media de la tarde.** |
| Tells Merche she will see her at 4:30 P.M. **Te veo a las cuatro y media.** | Says goodbye. **Adiós.** |

**17** Roberto and his friends Javier and Silvia are throwing a party this Saturday but they have to clean the house first. Look at the drawing and write the question Roberto's friends would use to ask what they should do. Then, take Roberto's place and write instructions to tell each friend what he or she needs to do. For example: **Debes limpiar la sala.**

Los amigos de Roberto preguntan: **¿Qué debemos hacer?**

Roberto dice: **Answers will vary. Possible Answers:**

**Debes planchar la ropa.**

**Debes limpiar la cocina.**

**Debes cuidar al gato.**

**18** When it comes to Calvin's duties and obligations, often Calvin and his parents have very different ideas. As you can see from the comic strip below, Calvin usually doesn't want to do what his parents want him to do.

Put yourself in the place of Calvin's mom, and imagine that you are trying to get him ready for school in the morning. What do you say to him? Write three recommendations or suggestions, using (**no**) **debes** + infinitive.

**Answers will vary.**

Now put yourself in Calvin's place. What do you think your mom should or should not do? Write three things you think Calvin might say, using (**no**) **debes** + infinitive.

**Answers will vary.**

# VAMOS A LEER

**19 a.** Below are three letters from the advice column in *Gente Joven*, a teen magazine. Read through the letters, using the reading strategies you've learned.

Querida *Gente Joven,*
Estoy desesperada y necesito su ayuda. Hay un chico en mi colegio que me gusta mucho. Se llama Francisco. Pero mis padres se oponen a° nuestra amistad°, porque piensan que es un muchacho "loco." Y ahora mis padres no me permiten hablar o salir con él. Pero quiero ser su amiga porque pienso que Francisco es una persona muy buena. ¿Qué debo hacer? **Cecilia**

**se oponen a** *are against, oppose*
**amistad** *friendship*

Querida *Gente Joven,*
Estoy preocupado por una amiga mía que se llama Elisa. Somos mejores amigos desde° el primer grado. Ahora Elisa está muy cambiada°. Ya no es la chica alegre, considerada, honesta, y trabajadora de antes. No estudia, no hace su tarea, no habla ni sale conmigo ni con sus otros amigos, siempre está cansada...su conducta no es la misma. Creo que tiene un problema muy grave, pero no sé qué hacer. **Diego**

**desde** *since*
**cambiada** *changed*

Querida *Gente Joven,*
Tengo 15 años y soy una chica responsable, madura e inteligente, pero mis padres son superestrictos conmigo. No me permiten usar el teléfono para llamar a mis amigos ni recibir llamadas°. No puedo salir durante la semana y sólo a veces los fines de semana. Mi vida es aburrida y triste. No sé por qué mis padres son así conmigo. Con mi hermano, no son tan estrictos. ¿Qué puedo hacer para ganar su confianza°? Gracias, **Amalia**

**llamadas** *phone calls*
**confianza** *confidence*

**b.** Answer the following questions.

1. What is the first letter about? A problem . . .
   **a.** at school (**b.**) with parents **c.** with a friend **d.** at work
2. What is the second letter about? A problem . . .
   **a.** with money **b.** with a brother/sister (**c.**) with a friend **d.** with parents
3. What is the third letter about? A problem . . .
   **a.** with a brother/sister **b.** with a teacher **c.** with a coach (**d.**) with parents
4. In the first letter, what do the parents think of Francisco? What does Cecilia think of him?
   **The parents think Francisco is "crazy". Cecilia thinks he's a great person.**
5. In the second letter, how is Elisa normally? And how has she been lately?
   **Elisa is normally thoughtful, honest, hardworking, cheerful. Lately she's hasn't been studying or doing her homework, talking or going out with friends, and she's always tired.**
6. In the third letter, how does Amalia describe herself? How does she compare her parents' treatment of her with the way her brother is treated?
   **She says she is responsible, mature and intelligent. She says her parents aren't so strict with her brother.**

**c.** You're a guest columnist for *Gente Joven*. Choose one letter to answer. Come up with at least three recommendations for solving the problem using **(no) debes** + infinitive.

**Answers will vary.**

Nombre ______________________ Clase ______________ Fecha ______________

# CULTURA

Muy Feliz Cumpleaños,
Comadre Querida
Muy Feliz Cumpleaños,
Querida Madrina

**20** As you read in the **Nota cultural** on p. 155 of your text, godparents are an important part of the Hispanic family. While the original function of godparents was to sponsor a child at its baptism and to take responsibility for its religious upbringing, today the **madrina** and **padrino** are also friends, advisors, and helpers to the child. They have very strong ties not only to their godchild, but also to the child's parents. The word **compadrazgo** literally means *joint paternity*. Mothers will refer to their child's godmother as **comadre** and fathers will call their child's godfather **compadre**, which also means *close friend*. Look over the greeting cards, and then work with a partner to answer the questions. Compare your answers with other classmates.

1. Can you figure out who the cards are for and what the occasion is?
   **Both are birthday cards for a godmother; the righthand card is from a godchild, and the other is from a godchild's mother.**

2. Are cards for godparents generally found in card stores in the U.S.? Why or why not?
   **Answers will vary.**

3. What does the fact that greeting cards exist especially for godparents tell you about their role in Spanish-speaking families?
   **Godparents are as important as other family members; their birthdays are celebrated as other family members' birthdays are.**

4. Why do you think that godparents play an important part in Hispanic family life?
   **Spanish-speaking families often have a strong Catholic background in which baptism and religious training are important. Spanish-speaking cultures also place a high value on friendship, and close friends are often friends from childhood through adulthood. The relationships between godchild and godparent and parent and comadre/compadre reflect these cultural values.**

5. Do you have godparents? What adults are close to and important to you?
   **Answers will vary.**

**21** What kinds of generalizations can you make about privacy in the U.S. and in Spanish-speaking countries?

**Answers will vary.**

CAPÍTULO 7

Nombre ______ Clase ______ Fecha ______

# ¿Qué te gustaría hacer?



## DE ANTEMANO

**1** Write the name of the **fotonovela** character next to each statement that he or she could have made. Choose from the following characters: Diego, Cristina, Pablo, or Sr. Andrade.

Diego 1. ¿Por qué Cristina no me invita a su fiesta? Somos buenos amigos...

Pablo 2. ¡Pobre Diego! Está muy triste. Me gustaría ayudar...

Cristina 3. ¡Qué pena! Pablo no puede ir a mi fiesta.

Sr. Andrade 4. ¿Dónde debo poner este recado para Diego? Ah... aquí en la mesa está bien.

Pablo 5. ¡Qué complicado! Me gustaría ir a la fiesta de Cristina, pero ya tengo planes con Diego.

**2** Greg, a new exchange student in Ecuador, has a really busy week planned. Based on his calendar below, match each invitation with the correct response.

| lunes | martes | miércoles | jueves | viernes | sábado | domingo |
|---|---|---|---|---|---|---|
| 4 | 5 | 6 | 7 | 8 | 9 | 10 |
| Reunión—club de intercambio, 6:00 p.m. | Cita—Dr. Londoño, 4:30 p.m. | Concierto, 9:30 p.m. | Cita—Oficina del Director, 10:00 a.m. | Examen de español, 9:00 a.m. | Fiesta—Cristina Ordóñez, 8:30 p.m. | Fútbol—parque, 12:30 p.m. |

e 1. ¿Quieres ir al cine esta noche a las seis?

a 2. ¿Cuándo es tu examen de español?

d 3. Vamos al zoológico este domingo. ¿Quieres ir también?

b 4. ¿Te gustaría venir a mi casa mañana después de clases?

f 5. Oye, vamos a tomar algo durante el descanso a las diez. ¿Quieres ir?

c 6. ¿Qué planes tienes para el sábado?

a. Es el viernes a las nueve. ¡Necesito estudiar y practicar mucho esta semana!

b. Lo siento, pero no puedo ir a tu casa. Mañana tengo una cita con el médico a las cuatro y media de la tarde.

c. El sábado por la noche voy a la fiesta de Cristina.

d. Creo que el domingo voy a jugar al fútbol. Pero gracias, ¿eh?

e. ¿A las seis? gracias, pero a las seis voy a una reunión del club de intercambio.

f. Lo siento, pero tengo una cita con el director a las diez.

Nombre ______________________ Clase ______________ Fecha ______________

# PRIMER PASO

**3** Below are parts of two phone conversations. Use the new words and expressions on p. 183 of your textbook to complete the missing parts of the conversations.

**Answers will vary. Possible answers:**

MANUEL ¿Aló?

ELENA 1. **Buenas tardes. ¿Está Leonor, por favor?**

MANUEL ¿De parte de quién, por favor?

ELENA 2. **Soy yo, Elena.**

MANUEL Elena ¿qué tal? Oye, lo siento, pero no está ahora.

ELENA 3. **¿Puedo dejar un recado?**

MANUEL Está bien.

Manuel

---

SRA. ALONSO 4. **Aló.; Diga.**

LEONOR Buenos días, Sra. Alonso. ¿Está Carmen, por favor?

SRA. ALONSO 5. **¿Quién habla?**

LEONOR Soy yo, Leonor.

SRA. ALONSO 6. **¿Cómo estás, Leonor?**

LEONOR Muy bien, gracias. ¿Y usted?

SRA. ALONSO 7. **Muy bien, gracias. Oye, Carmen no está ahora.**

LEONOR No hay problema. Llamo más tarde.

SRA. ALONSO 8. **Ella regresa a las cinco.**

LEONOR Bien. **Adiós**, Sra. Alonso.

SRA. ALONSO Adiós.

Leonor

**4** Sometimes Calvin answers the phone at his house and the results are not always what the callers expect. Read the following comic strip, then answer the questions.

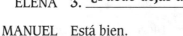

Nombre ______________________ Clase ____________ Fecha ____________



1. How does Calvin answer the phone? **¿Bueno?**
2. What are some other words used to answer the phone? **Alo; Diga.**
3. What does the caller want? **He wants to talk to Calvin's dad.**
4. Who do you think is calling in the last frame? **It's the same person, calling back.**
5. Imagine that the speech bubble in the third frame of the comic strip is empty. What could Calvin say in response to the caller's question that would be more helpful?
**Answers will vary. Possible answers: ¿De parte de quién, por favor?; ¿Quién habla, por favor?; Un momento, por favor.; ¿Quiere usted dejar un recado?**

**5** What would you invite the following people to do? Create an invitation for each one, based on what you think each person or group of people likes to do. Then write the other person's acceptance of the invitation. **Answers will vary. Possible answers:**

1. TÚ **¿Te gustaría ir al lago conmigo este fin de semana?**
TU AMIGO **¡Claro que sí! Me gusta pescar.**

2. TÚ **¿Les gustaría correr conmigo en el parque?**
TUS AMIGOS **Sí, nos gusta correr.**

3. TÚ **¿Les gustaría jugar al tenis esta tarde?**
TUS AMIGAS **¡Claro! Nos gustaría jugar contigo.**

4. TÚ **¿Te gustaría ir a un concierto mañana?**
TU AMIGO **Sí, me gusta escuchar música.**

5. TÚ **¿Quieren mirar la televisión esta noche conmigo?**
TUS AMIGOS **Sí, hay una película muy buena.**

Nombre ______________________ Clase ______________ Fecha ______________

**6** Use the clues and the **Vocabulario** section on p. 186 of your textbook to complete the following sentences.

1. El lugar donde puedes ver animales acuáticos es el **acuario**.
2. Un lugar donde viven muchas personas, por ejemplo, Quito o Miami, es una **ciudad**.
3. Cuando una persona termina las clases en el colegio, a veces hay una **fiesta de graduación** para celebrar.
4. Un lugar muy divertido, donde hay montañas rusas *(rollercoasters)*, es el **parque de atracciones**.
5. La ceremonia en que un hombre y una mujer se casan *(marry)* es una **boda**.
6. Una fiesta para celebrar 50 años de matrimonio *(marriage)* es una **fiesta de aniversario**.
7. El lugar lejos de las ciudades donde es posible ver la naturaleza *(nature)* es el **campo**.
8. Ahora tengo 14 años. En junio, voy a cumplir 15 y voy a tener una **fiesta de cumpleaños**.
9. El lugar donde puedes ver actores en una comedia es el **teatro**.
10. Vamos a celebrar el cumpleaños de Benjamín pero él no sabe (*doesn't know*) nada. Es una fiesta **de sorpresa**.

**7** Where would the people below rather go this weekend, and why? Write a sentence about each person's preferences based on the drawings.

MODELO

Mario prefiere ir al circo porque quiere ver los elefantes.

**Answers will vary. Possible answers:**

1. 

Esteban y Ramón

**Esteban y Ramón prefieren ir al parque de atracciones porque es muy divertido.**

2. 

El señor Arco

**El Sr. Arco prefiere ir al museo de antropología porque le gusta la historia.**

3. 

La familia Tamayo

**La familia Tamayo prefiere ir al zoológico porque a su hija le gustan los animales.**

4. 

Nosotros

**Nosotros preferimos ir al lago porque queremos nadar.**

# SEGUNDO PASO

**8** Some classmates are talking in the cafeteria about weekend plans. Read what each person has planned, then draw a line connecting the pairs of students that are going to do something together.

1. Más que nada, quiero ver los leones y los tigres, pero los elefantes son muy interesantes también.
2. Voy a pasar el sábado con mi amigo Felipe. Vamos al lago, ¡y nos vamos a divertir muchísimo!
3. Mi grupo favorito "Sabor tropical" va a tocar este sábado. ¡Son increíbles!
4. Antonio tiene dos entradas *(tickets)* para el nuevo parque de atracciones. Me encantan los parques de atracciones. ¡Pienso subir a la montaña rusa *(rollercoaster)* 50 veces!

a. Hay tantas cosas que hacer allí. Pienso nadar mucho.

b. Me gustaría mucho salir con Marisol este fin de semana. Ella quiere ir al parque de atracciones, pero a mí no me gusta la montaña rusa.

c. Mi prima Juanita y yo pensamos ir al zoológico el domingo. A ella le gustan mucho los animales.

d. Creo que Amalia y yo vamos a salir. Pensamos asistir a un concierto de música caribeña en el Teatro Central.

(Answers: 1–c, 2–a, 3–d, 4–b)

**9** Araceli and Manolo are planning what they're going to do this weekend. Complete their conversation with the correct forms of the following verbs.

**gustaría pensar tener querer ir venir preferir**

MANOLO Oye, Araceli, ¿qué **piensas** hacer este fin de semana?

ARACELI Pues, no sé. ¿Qué **vas** a hacer tú?

MANOLO Bueno, (yo) **quiero** ir al lago, pero mis hermanitos **quieren** jugar al tenis conmigo. Pero no me gusta mucho jugar al tenis; **prefiero/quiero** nadar. ¿Te **gustaría** ir al lago conmigo?

ARACELI Sí, me **gustaría**... pero, ¿cuándo **piensas** ir? **Prefiero/Quiero** ir el sábado porque el domingo por la tarde **voy** al museo con Guillermo.

MANOLO ¿**Vienes** a mi casa a las tres el sábado?

ARACELI Primero **tengo** tarea, pero a las tres no hay problema.

Nombre ______________________ Clase ____________ Fecha ____________

**10** Emilio is talking to Alejandra about weekend plans. Using the expressions **ir** + **a** + infinitive and **pensar** + infinitive, write what Emilio would say about his and his friends' plans.

MODELO

Amador

Amador va a ir al parque este fin de semana. Piensa jugar al fútbol con sus amigos.

**Answers will vary. Possible answers:**

Emilio

1. **Voy a ir a un restaurante mexicano este fin de semana. Pienso cenar con mi amiga Teresa.**

Alejandra

2. **Alejandra tiene planes para este fin de semana. Piensa ir al lago.**

Víctor

3. **Víctor no va a salir de casa este fin de semana. Piensa descansar.**

Rafa y José Luis

4. **Rafa y José Luis van a ir al parque de atracciones este fin de semana. Piensan hacer muchas cosas divertidas.**

**11** This Saturday Gustavo has a lot of plans. Write at least five sentences describing his day, using the illustrations as a guide and the expressions in the box below.

**ir + a + ...**
**pensar + ...**
**necesitar + ...**
**querer + ...**
**A Gustavo le gustaría + ...**

**Answers will vary.**

**12** The Montemayors are going out with some friends tonight. Complete the following sentences with what each person needs to do to get ready according to the cues. Start with Mrs. Montemayor asking her husband if everyone is ready.

1. ¿Están todos **listos** ?
2.  No, mi amor. Marco **necesita lavarse los dientes.**
3.  Y yo **necesito afeitarme.**
4.  Creo que tú **necesitas maquillarte.**
5.  Luego Marisa **necesita peinarse.**
6.  Y por último, Pepe **necesita ducharse.**

Nombre ______________________ Clase __________ Fecha __________

# TERCER PASO

**13** The strip below shows a conversation between Calvin and his friend Susi. Read the cartoon, then answer the questions.

| | | | |
|---|---|---|---|
| **el té** | *tea* | **secuestrado** | *kidnapped* |
| **Estoy buscando** | *I'm looking for* | **un grosero** | *a rude person* |

1. Hobbes is Calvin's toy tiger. What is Hobbes "doing" in the strip above?
   **Hobbes is having tea with Susi and her toy rabbit.**
2. What phrase does Susi use in the second scene to extend an invitation to Calvin ?
   **¿No quieres venir a tomar el té?**
3. What's his answer and why do you think he answers this way?
   **He says no because he's busy looking for Hobbes.**
4. What does Susi think of Calvin because of the way he answered?
   **She thinks he's rude.**

**14** How else could Calvin have responded to Susi's invitation? Imagine that you are the cartoonist, and create three new responses for Calvin. Look at page 193 of your textbook for reference.

**Answers will vary.**

a. an acceptance

______________________

b. a refusal with an explanation

______________________

c. a suggestion that he and Susi do something else

______________________

**15** Luisa and Marcos were passing notes to each other in study hall. Match up what Marcos wrote on the left with Luisa's sentences on the right. Number Luisa's sentences in the correct order to find out what they were discussing. When you finish, read through the note in order and answer the questions below.

| Marcos | | Luisa |
|---|---|---|
| 1. ¿Qué vas a hacer este sábado? | 4 | Bueno, ¿te gustaría estudiar conmigo? A mí me gustan las matemáticas. |
| 3. Porque tengo que hacer la tarea de matemáticas y es muy difícil. | 8 | Buena idea... siempre tengo ganas de comer algo después de estudiar. |
| 5. ¿En serio? Gracias... me gustaría mucho. ¿A qué hora quieres estudiar? | 2 | Por la mañana, nada, pero por la tarde, voy a salir. ¿Por qué? |
| 7. ¡Perfecto! Y después, si quieres, vamos a comer una hamburguesa. | 6 | ¿Por qué no vienes a mi casa a las diez? Así podemos estudiar juntos. |

**16** Create a conversation between you and your best friend. Invite him or her to two different places. Your friend declines the first invitation but accepts the second idea. Decide on a time and place to meet. Use the following expressions in your conversation.

vas a... piensas...
te gustaría... quieres...

_______________________________________________
_______________________________________________
_______________________________________________
_______________________________________________
_______________________________________________
_______________________________________________
_______________________________________________
_______________________________________________
_______________________________________________
_______________________________________________

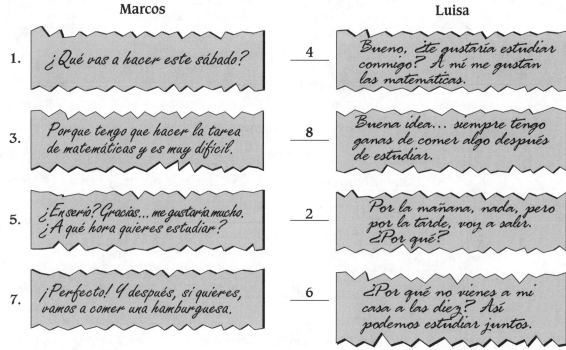

Nombre ______________________ Clase ______________ Fecha ______________

**17** Joaquín has just called some friends to come over and watch videos this afternoon. Based on what you see in the pictures, how do his friends respond? Include Joaquín's invitation and his friends' excuses in each conversation. Use the following expressions: **tener que** + infinitive, **tener sueño**, **(no) tener ganas de** + infinitive, and **tener prisa**.

**Jimena**

**Juanito**

**Fernanda**

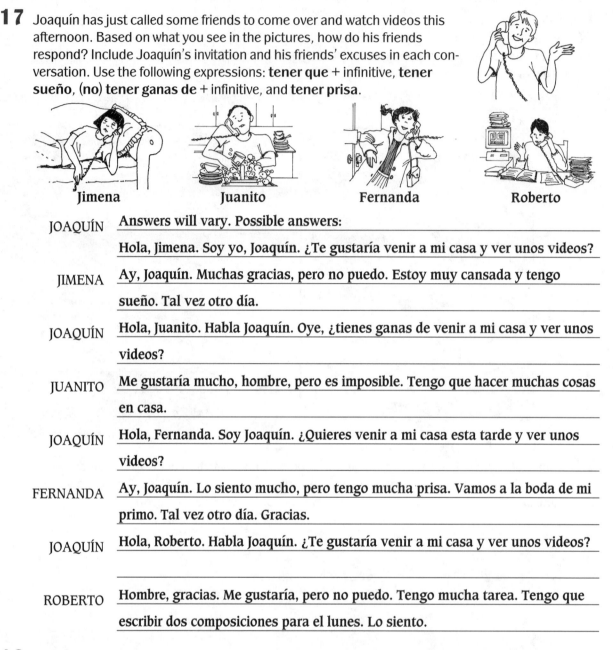

**Roberto**

JOAQUÍN **Answers will vary. Possible answers:**
**Hola, Jimena. Soy yo, Joaquín. ¿Te gustaría venir a mi casa y ver unos videos?**

JIMENA **Ay, Joaquín. Muchas gracias, pero no puedo. Estoy muy cansada y tengo sueño. Tal vez otro día.**

JOAQUÍN **Hola, Juanito. Habla Joaquín. Oye, ¿tienes ganas de venir a mi casa y ver unos videos?**

JUANITO **Me gustaría mucho, hombre, pero es imposible. Tengo que hacer muchas cosas en casa.**

JOAQUÍN **Hola, Fernanda. Soy Joaquín. ¿Quieres venir a mi casa esta tarde y ver unos videos?**

FERNANDA **Ay, Joaquín. Lo siento mucho, pero tengo mucha prisa. Vamos a la boda de mi primo. Tal vez otro día. Gracias.**

JOAQUÍN **Hola, Roberto. Habla Joaquín. ¿Te gustaría venir a mi casa y ver unos videos?**

ROBERTO **Hombre, gracias. Me gustaría, pero no puedo. Tengo mucha tarea. Tengo que escribir dos composiciones para el lunes. Lo siento.**

**18** You have been invited to a graduation party, and you're really looking forward to it. Write a short paragraph including: what you plan to do at the party, what you feel and don't feel like doing at the party, and what you have to do to get ready for the party. Use the following verb expressions.

**Tengo que** **Quiero** **Voy a** **Me gustaría** **Pienso** **Necesito** **Tengo ganas de**

**Answers will vary.**

# VAMOS A LEER

**19** In the U.S., we tend to take having a phone for granted. However, in some parts of Spain and Latin America, having a telephone in one's home can be the exception rather than the rule. Residents may be put on a long waiting list to have a phone line installed and to get a telephone. Also both local and long-distance calls are extremely expensive. For these reasons, it is not unusual for people in Spanish-speaking countries to use public phone booths or **Telefónicas** *(calling centers)* instead of having a phone at home.

Knowing a little about phones in Spanish-speaking countries can help you understand the reading. Here is a page from a phone book. Look it over, then answer the questions below.

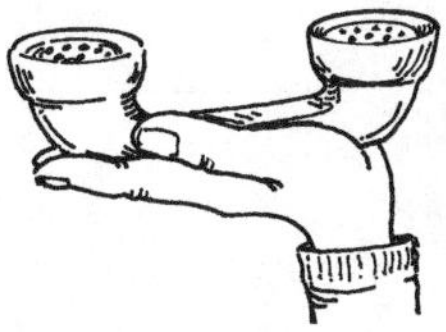

**1.**
**El teléfono es una parte importante de la vida. Aprécielo en todo su valor.**

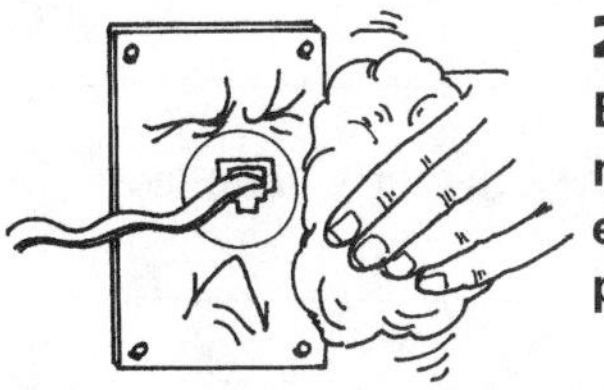

**2.**
**El bloque de conexión de su teléfono es delicado. Hay que protegerlo.**

**3.**
**El teléfono no es un juguete. Controle su uso.**

**4.**
**Sus hijos no deben hacer su tarea por teléfono. Use el teléfono en forma mesurada.**

**5.**
**No debe monopolizar el teléfono de la oficina. Sea breve.**

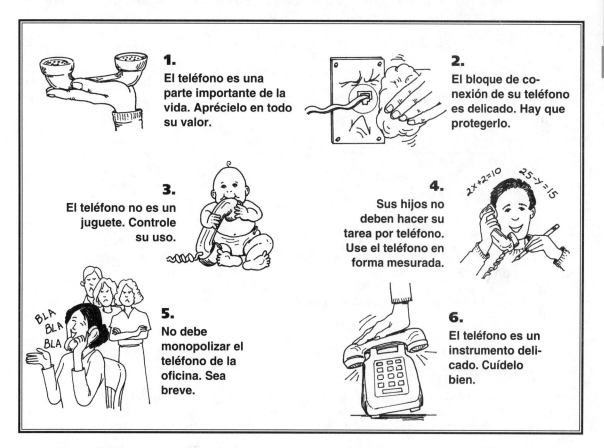

**6.**
**El teléfono es un instrumento delicado. Cuídelo bien.**

1. What is this information about?
   a. how to get directory assistance
   (b.) how to use phones properly

2. Look at number 3. Based on the drawing, what do you think this rule is saying?
   (a.) phones are not toys
   b. babies can play with the phone as long as no one needs to use it

3. What do numbers 1, 2, and 6 all have in common?
   a. they say that the telephone is part of modern life
   (b.) they urge taking care of the phone and the phone connections

4. Numbers 4 and 5 are also similar. What do they all recommend doing?
   (a.) keeping phone conversations at home and at work brief
   b. talking on the phone for a long time at night when the rates are lowest

Nombre ______________________ Clase ____________ Fecha ____________

# CULTURA

**20** As you read in the **Nota cultural** on p. 189 of your textbook, public transportation is a bigger part of day-to-day life in Spanish-speaking countries than in the U.S. It's not uncommon in larger cities, such as Buenos Aires, Madrid, or Mexico City, for people not to own a car, but to rely instead on the subway or bus systems for transportation. In Spain, the subway is called **el metro**, while in Buenos Aires, it's referred to as **el subte** (short for **el subterráneo**). A public bus in Uruguay and Argentina is **un colectivo** or **un ómnibus**, **una guagua** in Puerto Rico and Cuba, and **un autobús** in Spain. Answer the questions below, in English.

1. How do you generally get to school, to work, and to after-school activities? How do you get around on the weekends?

   **Answers will vary.**

2. Do you have a driver's license and access to a car?

3. Is there a bus or subway system where you live? Do you ever use it? Why or why not?

4. What are the advantages and disadvantages of using a car as your main means of transportation?

5. What are the advantages and disadvantages of getting around using a public transportation system?

6. Can you imagine living in your area without a car? What would you do instead?

**21** Now imagine that you're a student living in Buenos Aires, the capital city of Argentina and you don't have a car. Describe how you get around. What are some advantages and disadvantages?

**Answers will vary.**

Nombre ______________ Clase ______________ Fecha ______________

CAPÍTULO 8

# ¡A comer!

## DE ANTEMANO

**1** Who orders what in the **fotonovela**? Look over the story on pp. 204–205 of your textbook, then match each character with what he or she orders.

Diego

Chen

empanadas

plátanos

agua

sancocho

carne colorada

legumbres

Cristina

Raúl

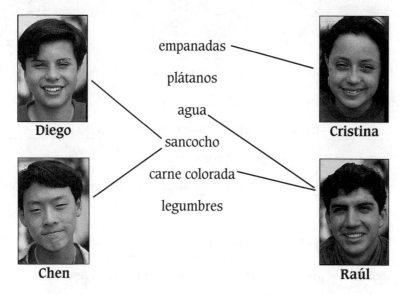

**2** Match the different characters' questions on the left with answers on the right. Write the letter of the best response to each question in the blank.

e 1. Raúl, ¿qué es carne colorada?

d 2. Cristina, ¿por qué no vas a pedir el sancocho?

f 3. Diego, ¿no quieres otro sancocho?

a 4. Bueno, Chen... ¿qué tal está el sancocho?

c 5. Tengo sed todavía. ¿Vamos a pedir otra botella de agua?

a. Está riquísimo. ¿Quieres un poco?

b. ¡Cuidado! La sopa está muy caliente.

c. ¿Por qué no pides dos? El ají aquí está super-picante.

d. Porque comemos sancocho en casa casi todas las semanas. Hoy quiero empanadas.

e. Es un plato de carne, muy típico del Ecuador... a mí me encanta.

f. No, gracias. Está muy bueno, pero no puedo comer más.

# PRIMER PASO

**3** Breakfast at the Montalvo house is often complicated because each person likes to have something different. Using each drawing, write a sentence saying what each member of the family has for breakfast.

1. 
Raquel y Esteban

2. 
Luis

3. 
Sr. Montalvo

4. 
Sra. Montalvo

1. **Para el desayuno, ellos comen cereal, pan tostado y beben un vaso de jugo.**
2. **Por lo general, Luis come pan dulce, unos plátanos y bebe un vaso de leche.**
3. **El señor Montalvo come huevos con tocino y bebe café.**
4. **A la Sra. Montalvo le gusta comer toronja. También toma café con leche y pan dulce.**

**4** Breakfast is the most important meal of the day, but not everyone eats a good breakfast. What nutritional advice do you have for the following people? Based on each person's comments, write one or two sentences telling each one what he or she should eat for breakfast.

MODELO Nunca tomo desayuno. Por las mañanas siempre tengo prisa.
**Si siempre tienes prisa, debes comer uno o dos plátanos, pan tostado y tomar un vaso de leche.**

1. DIANA Estoy a dieta, y por eso no desayuno nunca.
TÚ **Answers will vary.**

2. CHEMA ¡Uf! No me gusta comer por las mañanas.
TÚ ______________________

3. EUGENIA Me gustan mucho los huevos y el tocino... pero tienen mucho colesterol.
TÚ ______________________

4. DIEGO Soy alérgico a *(allergic to)* la leche y el yogurt.
TÚ ______________________

5. CHUY El médico dice que necesito comer más fruta fresca.
TÚ ______________________

6. MARÍA ¡Siempre lo mismo! Cereal con leche. Quiero comer algo más interesante de vez en cuando.
TÚ ______________________

Nombre ______________________ Clase ____________ Fecha ____________

**5** How do you feel about the following foods? Explain how often you eat them, using **encantar** and **gustar**. Then tell why you like or don't like each one. Is there a food that you really don't like at all? Write about it in number 7.

1.  **Answers will vary.**

2. 

3. 

4. 

5. 

6. 

7. **¡No me gusta(n) ... para nada!**

**6** It's late morning and everyone's hungry and thinking about his or her favorite lunch. Write what each of the people in the picture love to have for lunch, using one of the expressions from the box.
**Answers will vary. Possible answers:**

| encantar | comer | preferir | gustar |
|---|---|---|---|

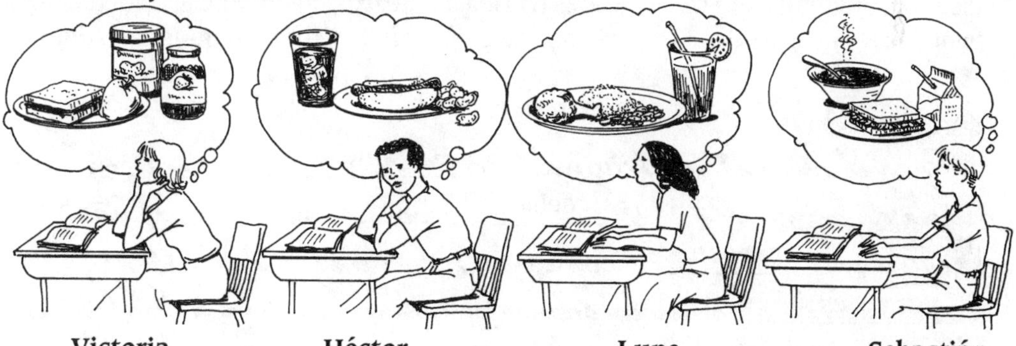

**Victoria** **Héctor** **Lupe** **Sebastián**

1. **A Victoria le encanta comer un sándwich de crema de maní y jalea y una manzana para el almuerzo.**
2. **Héctor prefiere comer un perro caliente, unas papitas y un té frío.**
3. **A Lupe le gusta mucho almorzar arroz y pollo y un vaso de limonada.**
4. **Por lo general, Sebastián come sopa de pollo, un sándwich de jamón y jugo de naranja.**

Nombre ______________________ Clase ____________ Fecha ____________

**7** A Spanish-speaking magazine is doing a survey to find out more about the eating habits of high-school students. Take part in the survey by completing the questionnaire below.

## Cuestionario, 1a parte

1. Cuando estoy enfermo(a), me encanta(n)... **Answers will vary.**
2. Por lo general, no me gusta(n) para nada... ______
3. Para el desayuno, me encanta tomar... ______
4. Después del almuerzo, me encanta comer... ______
5. Antes de dormir me encanta comer... ______
6. Cuando salgo con mis amigos, nos encanta comer... ______
7. Los domingos por la mañana me encanta tomar... ______
8. Por lo general, almuerzo a las... ______



**8** Luisa is babysitting and Sra. Benavides has left a note explaining what each of the Benavides children can and can't eat. Complete her note with forms of the verb **poder** and **deber**.

*Querida Luisa,*

*Para el almuerzo, Miguelito* 1. **puede** *comer un sándwich de crema de maní. No* 2. **debe** *comer muchas papitas. Susanita y Carlitos* 3. **pueden** *comer la sopa de verduras. Y tú* 4. **puedes** *comer la sopa o comer un sándwich también. De postre todos* 5. **pueden** *comer fruta.*

*Para la cena, Susanita no* 6. **debe** *comer el pollo porque tiene alergias. Ella* 7. **puede** *comer una hamburguesa. Carlitos y Miguelito* 8. **pueden** *comer el pollo o los espaguetis. De postre, tú* 9. **puedes** *comer helado, si quieres... ¡pero los niños no* 10. **deben** *comer mucho helado!*

*Si tienes un problema,* 11. **puedes** *hablar con la vecina, la señora Aguirre.*

*Buena suerte con todo, y gracias.*

*Sra. Benavides*

Nombre ______________________ Clase ____________ Fecha ____________

# SEGUNDO PASO

**9** Everyone has a particular food that he or she can't stand. Read the following cartoon to find out what it is that Juanito hates.

**¡Guácala! ¡Qué asco!** *Yuck! Gross!*
**¿Ya terminaste las coles de Bruselas?** *Have you finished your Brussels sprouts?*

How would Juanito answer the question **¿Cómo están las coles de Bruselas?** Circle the number of each sentence below that matches Juanito's reaction to his dinner.

1. "Están deliciosas."
2. "No me gustan para nada estas coles de Bruselas ."
3. "Estas coles de Bruselas están frías y saladas."
4. "¡Uf! No puedo comer estas coles de Bruselas."
5. "Las coles de Bruselas de mi mamá siempre están muy ricas."
6. "Me encanta comer en esta casa."

**10** What would you ask or say in the following situations? Using phrases from p. 212 of your textbook and other phrases you know, write two or three sentences to respond to each situation. Be honest, but remember to be polite!

1. You and your friend have swapped lunches today. When you bite into his sandwich, you realize that it has hot peppers. **Answers will vary. Possible answers:**

   **¡Está muy picante!**

2. For your mom's birthday, you've made her favorite meal. You want to know what she thinks of the main course and dessert.

   **¿Cómo está el/la...? ¿Y cómo está el postre?**

3. As a surprise, your friend makes home-made ice cream for your birthday.

   **Está frío y dulce.**

4. The waiter at your favorite restaurant asks how your chicken soup is.

   **¿Cómo está la sopa de pollo?**

5. When you come home from school, someone's been baking and the kitchen is full of chocolate chip cookies.
**Las galletas están deliciosas.**

**11** Look at the **Nota gramatical** on p. 212 of your textbook. Remember that **ser** is used to describe general or typical characteristics of a food. **Estar** is used to describe how particular dishes taste, seem, or look. For each English sentence below, choose the form of **ser** or **estar** to complete the Spanish equivalent.

MODELO These cookies taste great.
**Estas galletas (son/<u>están</u>) muy ricas.**
Here **están** is the right answer, because the sentence is talking about how these cookies taste, not what cookies in general are like.

1. Soup is good when you're sick.
**La sopa (<u>es</u> /está) buena cuando estás enfermo/a.**
2. Careful! This pizza is really hot!
**¡Cuidado! Esta pizza (es /<u>está</u>) muy caliente.**
3. Yuck! The spaghetti is cold.
**¡Qué asco! Los espaguetis (son /<u>están</u>) fríos.**
4. Mexican food is spicy, right?
**La comida mexicana (<u>es</u> /está) picante, ¿verdad?**
5. I love chocolate ice cream. It's delicious.
**Me encanta el helado de chocolate. (<u>Es</u> /Está) muy rico.**
6. Hmm . . . this jelly doesn't taste very sweet.
**Mmm... esta jalea no (es /<u>está</u>) muy dulce.**
7. Milk is good for children.
**La leche (<u>es</u> /está) buena para los chicos.**



**12** In this chapter you've learned how to say more things with the verb **tener**. Do you remember other expressions with **tener** as well? Describe each of the following pictures using at least three expressions with **tener**.

1. **Arturo**

**Answers will vary. Possible answers:**
**Arturo tiene sed. Tiene ganas de tomar una limonada. Tiene prisa porque tiene que ir al colegio.**

Nombre ______________________ Clase ____________ Fecha ____________

2. Celia

**Celia tiene sueño y tiene ganas de descansar pero tiene que estudiar. También tiene hambre.**

**13** You want to take a survey on eating habits of high school students. Complete this set of questions by asking what students eat or drink

1) when they're hungry or thirsty after class
2) when they're in a hurry
3) when they need a quick lunch

## Cuestionario, 2a parte

1. Cuando tengo mucha sed después de clase, me gusta tomar... ____________
2. Cuando tengo mucha hambre, a veces como... ____________
3. Por lo general, cuando tengo prisa me gusta comer... ____________
4. Mi almuerzo favorito cuando necesito algo rápido es... ____________
5. Por la noche, siempre tengo ganas de comer... ____________
6. Si no tengo sueño, por lo general puedo dormir después de tomar... ____________
7. Si no tengo mucha hambre para el desayuno, como... ____________

Nombre ______________________ Clase ______________ Fecha ______________

# TERCER PASO

**14** Find out what seven items you need to set the table by placing the syllables in the correct order. Then write the words out below.

**cu so vi ta pla lle ne cha zón cu to ta llo te chi ra ser dor va**

Necesito una ___cuchara___, un ___cuchillo___, un ___plato___, una ___servilleta___, un ___tazón___, un ___vaso___ y un ___tenedor___.

**15** Look over the vocabulary for this chapter to complete the crossword puzzle below.

**Horizontales**

2. La primera comida del día.
6. Una comida que se come *(is eaten)* con jalea en un sándwich.
9. Unos mariscos *(shellfish)* pequeños.
10. Una bebida con mucha vitamina C.
11. Una bebida fría que se hace con limones.
12. Un tipo de legumbre anaranjada.
13. La lista de comidas en un restaurante se llama el ___.
14. La cosa que se usa *(is used)* para limpiar la boca *(mouth)* después de comer.
15. Una legumbre verde y un ingrediente importante en una ensalada.

**Verticales**

1. Antes de pagar en un restaurante, necesitas pedir la ___.
3. La comida después del desayuno.
4. Una fruta cítrica, más grande que *(bigger than)* una naranja.
5. La comida después del almuerzo.
7. Una agua especial que se sirve *(is served)* en botellas.
8. El atún y el salmón son tipos de ___.
9. La hamburguesa se hace *(is made)* con ___.

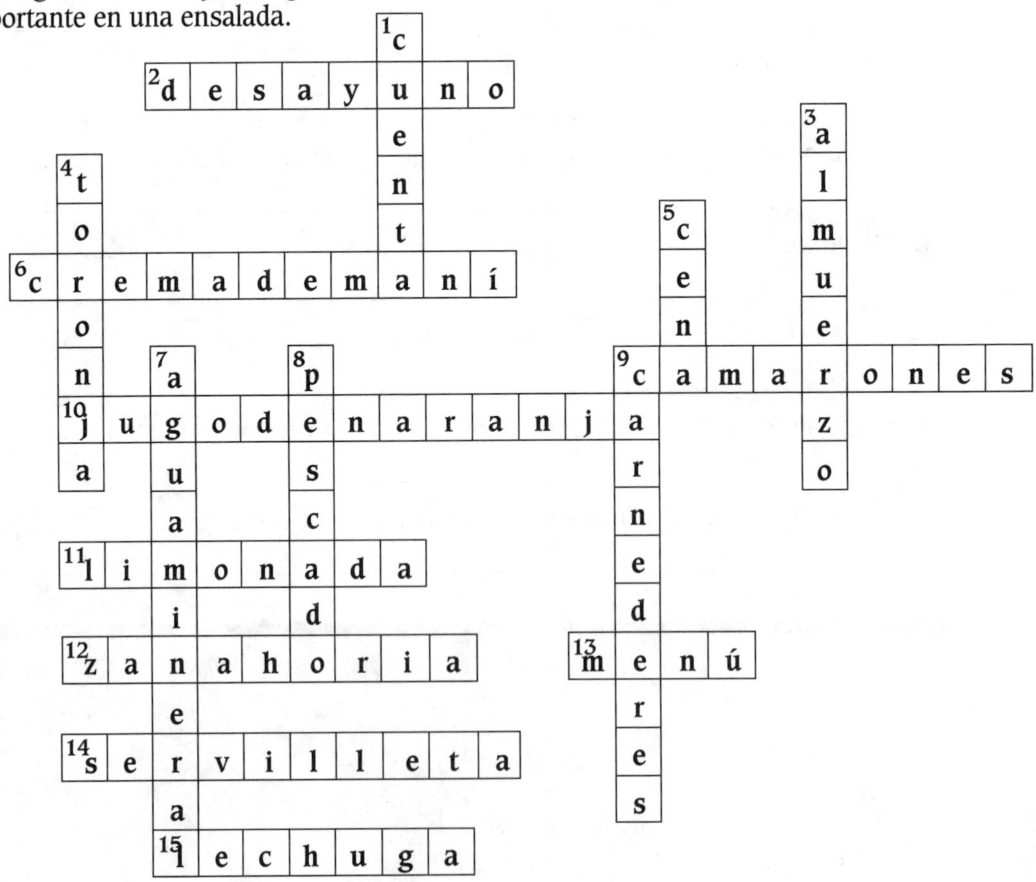

**16** You're at the **Café El Rincón** for dinner with a large group of friends. It's your waiter's first day on the job, and he keeps making mistakes with everyone's order. All of the things pictured below are things that he needs to bring you. How would you politely ask for them?

**Answers will vary. Possible answers:**

1. 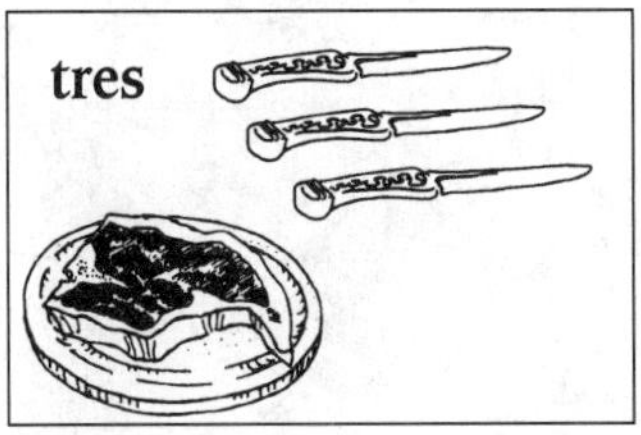


**Camarero, ¿nos puede traer tres cuchillos y un bistec por favor?**

2. 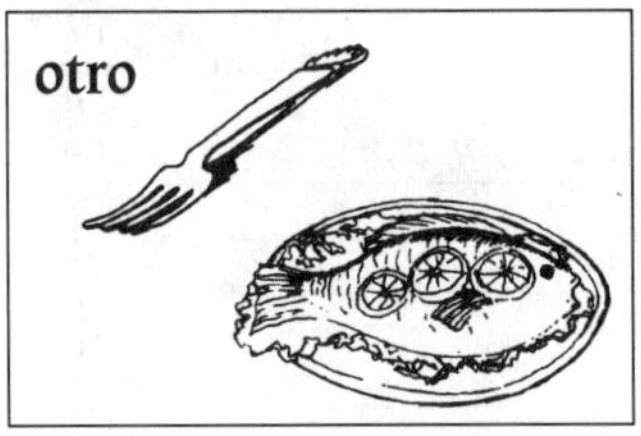


**¿Me trae otro tenedor y el pescado por favor?**

3. 

**Camarero, ¿nos puede traer agua mineral y un vaso por favor?**

4. 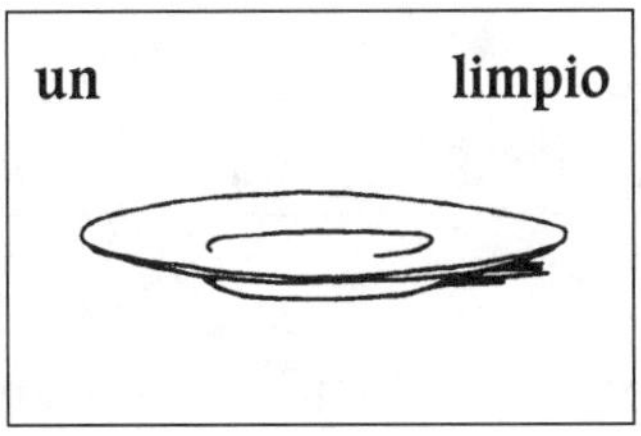


**Camarero, ¿me trae un plato limpio? Este plato está sucio.**

5. 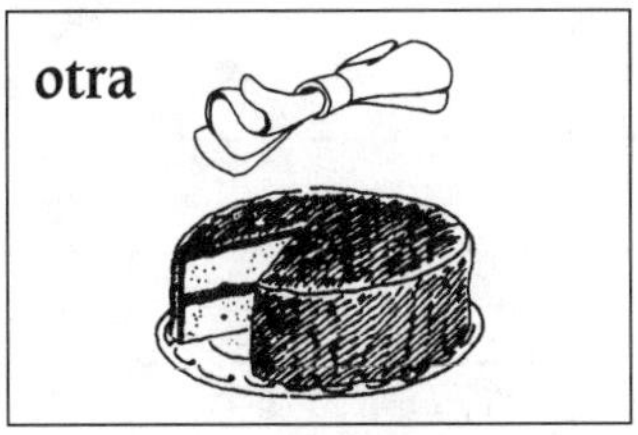


**Camarero, ¿nos puede traer otra servilleta y el pastel por favor?**

6. 

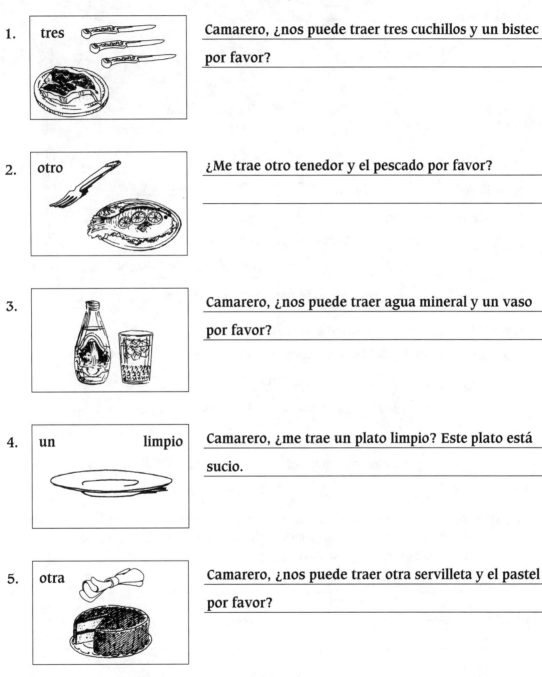

**Camarero, ¿me trae otra cuchara y un tazón/plato hondo de helado por favor?**

Nombre ____________________ Clase __________ Fecha __________

**17** Manuel, Marimar and Sofía are eating out to celebrate Marimar's birthday. Fill in the dialogue according to what takes place in the illustration.

**Answers will vary. Possible answers:**

SOFÍA Bueno, Marimar, ¿qué **vas a pedir**?

MARIMAR **Voy** a pedir **el pescado con zanahorias y maíz.**

SOFÍA Debes pedir una ensalada también. Ah, aquí viene la camarera.

CAMARERA **Buenas tardes. ¿Qué les puedo traer?**

SOFÍA ¿Para mí? Bueno, yo **quisiera el arroz con verduras y pollo, por favor.**

MARIMAR A mí **me trae el pescado con zanahorias y maíz**. Ah, y **una ensalada**, también.

CAMARERA Muy bien. Y a usted señor, ¿qué le **puedo** traer?

MANUEL **Para mí, el bistec con papas fritas y una ensalada, por favor.**

CAMARERA Muy bien. ¿Y qué les **gustaría** de tomar?

SOFÍA **¿Nos puede traer tres aguas minerales, por favor?**

CAMARERA ¿Desean algo más? ¿Algún postre?

SOFÍA **Sí, queremos pastel y helado de chocolate, por favor.**

**18** Finish the conversation between the group of friends and the waitress. Sofía wants to know the amount of the bill and if the tip is included. Manuel asks for the bill; the waitress brings it and wishes her customers a good evening.

SOFÍA **Answers will vary.**

CAMARERA ____________________

SOFÍA ____________________

CAMARERA ____________________

MANUEL ____________________

CAMARERA ____________________

Nombre ______________________ Clase ____________ Fecha ____________

# VAMOS A LEER

**19** As you read in the **Nota cultural** on p. 210 of your textbook, lunch (**la comida**) is the main meal of the day in Spanish-speaking countries. It usually consists of a lighter **primer plato** *(first course)* of soup, pasta, vegetables, etc., and is followed by a more substantial **segundo plato** *(main course)* of meat, chicken, or fish. Dessert, often consisting of fresh fruit, is also part of the meal. If this type of lunch seems like a lot of food to you, remember that most Spanish speakers have lighter breakfasts and dinners than we do in the U.S.

Below is a restaurant menu from Spain. As part of the **menú del día** *(daily specials)*, diners choose one **primer plato** and one **segundo plato**, plus **postre** *(dessert)*, in any combination, for a fixed price. Look over the menu, then answer the questions below.

Menú del día 1100 pesetas
Pan, agua o vino y postre incluidos

1er plato
Espaguetis
Ensalada mixta
Sopa de fideos° — *noodles*
Tortilla° de jamón — *omelet*

2ndo plato
Filete de bistec
Bonito° con tomate — *tuna*
Pollo asado° — *roasted*
Gambas al ajillo° — *shrimp in garlic sauce*

Postre
Arroz con leche° — *rice pudding*
Fruta del tiempo
Helados variados

1. Which dishes from the **1er plato** group have pasta? Do any dishes have meat? If so, which ones?

   **The spaghetti and the noodle soup; yes, the ham omelet**

2. What are the seafood dishes in the **2ndo plato** group? If you didn't like seafood, what could you have instead as your second course?

   **The shrimp and tuna; you could have roasted chicken or beef**

3. What would be a good **1er plato** to eat if it's cold outside? if it's hot outside?

   **The noodle soup; the salad**

4. Look at the choices under **Postre**. What do you think the words **del tiempo** mean when referring to fruit? What does **helados variados** tell you about the assortment of flavors of ice cream this restaurant has?

   **In season; there are many different flavors**

# CULTURA

**20** While cereal is the most popular breakfast food in the U.S., it's not as common in Spanish-speaking countries. As you read in the **Nota cultural** on p. 209 of your textbook, breakfast in most Spanish-speaking countries is pretty light. Besides the foods mentioned in your textbook, people will often have **galletas** (crispy, not-too-sweet cookies, sort of like graham crackers) or **magdalenas** (small sweet rolls that taste like pound cake) with breakfast, dunking them in their coffee, chocolate, or milk. If this seems like a skimpy breakfast to you, remember that it's common for people to have a mid-morning **merienda**, or snack, at about 10:00 or 11:00 to tide them over until lunch.

**a.** Compare breakfast in your house and what you know about breakfast in Spanish-speaking countries. Which style of breakfast do you like better, and why?

**Answers will vary.**

**b.** Which seems healthier to you? What are the advantages and disadvantages of each?



**21** Look at the **Nota cultural** on p. 214 of your textbook. You may have been surprised to learn that Ecuadorean food is not spicy. In the U.S., a common belief is that food in all Spanish-speaking countries is similar to the spicy dishes of Mexico. Such beliefs about food go both ways. For example, many people in other countries believe that everyone in the U.S. eats fast food all the time.

**a.** In your opinion, is **la comida norteamericana** really just fast food, or is it something else? Explain.

**Answers will vary.**

**b.** Now make a list of five or six breakfast, lunch, dinner, or dessert dishes that you would recommend to a Spanish-speaking tourist who wants to try some "American food."

**22** How would you like to go home at midday, eat with your family, and take a short nap or watch TV before going back to classes? While the idea might seem strange to you, it's part of the everyday routine for many students in Spanish-speaking countries, and to them, what you do and eat at lunchtime might seem unusual. Briefly describe your lunchtime routine and compare it to the routine described above. If you could choose, which routine would you rather have?

**Answers will vary.**

CAPÍTULO 9

Nombre ______________ Clase ______________ Fecha ______________

# ¡Vamos de compras!

## DE ANTEMANO

**1** As the three friends from the **fotonovela** go shopping, they ask each other a lot of questions. Can you match up each question with the most logical answer below?

__e__ 1. ¿Qué le gusta a Héctor?

__b__ 2. Héctor practica muchos deportes, ¿verdad?

__a__ 3. ¿Qué te parece esta blusa?

__f__ 4. Oye, ¿cuánto cuestan esos bluejeans?

__c__ 5. Podemos comprarle un libro, ¿no?

a. Me parece muy elegante... pero es un poco cara, ¿no?
b. Sí, tal vez podemos regalarle unos zapatos de tenis.
c. Ya tiene muchísimos libros. Prefiero regalarle algo más original.
d. ¡Buena idea! La zapatería está aquí al lado.
e. Le gusta prácticamente todo... escuchar música, ir al cine, bailar, salir...
f. Cuestan $40.00. ¡Qué caros!

**2** Decide whether each of the following statements is **cierto** (c) or **falso** (f) according to the **fotonovela**.

__f__ 1. Héctor quiere comprarles un regalo a las tres chicas para su graduación.

__c__ 2. Eva, Lisa y Gabi van a la tienda de ropa nada más para mirar.

__f__ 3. Las tres chicas compran muchas cosas en la tienda de ropa.

__c__ 4. A Gabi le gusta la falda de algodón. Dice que es una ganga.

__f__ 5. Gabi piensa comprarle un libro a Héctor.

__c__ 6. Cada una de las tres chicas le compra el mismo regalo a Héctor.

Nombre ____________________ Clase ____________ Fecha ____________

# PRIMER PASO

**3** Emily is asking Esteban what gifts he plans to give different members of his family. First write Emily's questions, using the picture cues below and expressions from **Así se dice** on page 237 of your textbook. Then go back and write Esteban's answers to each question.

**Abuelo** **Abuela** **Papá** **Mamá** **Luisito** **Maripili**

Emily wants to know...

1. whom the wallet is for **¿Para quién es la cartera?/**
   **(La cartera) Es para Luisito.**
2. what Esteban plans to buy for his sister **¿Qué piensas comprarle (regalarle) a tu hermana?/Pienso regalarle (comprarle) un juego de mesa.**
3. what type of gift he is looking for his grandfather **¿Qué tipo de regalo buscas para tu abuelo?/Busco una corbata.**
4. whom the earrings are for **¿Para quién son los aretes?/**
   **(Los aretes) Son para mi abuela.**
5. what Esteban plans to give his mom **¿Qué piensas regalarle a tu mamá?/**
   **Pienso regalarle una planta.**
6. whom the compact disc is for **¿Para quién es el disco compacto?/**
   **(El disco compacto) Es para papá.**

**4** Read the descriptions of some of María's friends. Based on what you find out, what gift do you think María is going to give to each of them? Follow the model. **Answers will vary.**

MODELO A Amalia le encantan las películas viejas.
**María le va a regalar un video de una película de John Wayne.**

1. A su amigo Tomás le gusta la ropa formal.
   **María le va a dar una corbata.**
2. A su amiga Margarita le encantan las joyas (*jewelry*).
   **Le va a regalar un collar o unos aretes.**

3. A Juan Pedro y a Mario les encanta la música. Escuchan música todo el tiempo.
   **Les va a regalar unos discos compactos.**

4. Su amiga Olga está enferma.
   **A Olga le va a dar unas flores y una tarjeta.**

5. A Antonio le gusta mucho trabajar en el jardín.
   **Le va a dar una planta.**

6. Sus primos Miguelito y Javier sólo tienen seis y cinco años.
   **A ellos les va a comprar unos juguetes.**

**5** Fill in the word puzzle with the words defined below. If you complete the puzzle correctly, in the vertical column you will find the answer to the question **¿Qué buscas en el centro comercial?**

1. El tipo de tienda donde puedes comprar caramelos.
2. En esta tienda grande, hay de todo: ropa, televisores, camas, escritorios... ¡todo!
3. Para comprar comida, puedes ir a una tienda de ___.
4. En esta tienda puedes comprar comida, y también cosméticos, detergentes, plantas y otras cosas.
5. El tipo de tienda donde puedes comprar galletas, pasteles y pan dulce.
6. Para comprar pan, debes ir a una ___.
7. Para comprar una novela o una revista, necesitas ir a una ___.
8. Si te gustan los aretes y los collares, tu tienda favorita es la ___.
9. Es la tienda favorita de los niños pequeños.
10. Si necesitas unos zapatos de tenis, vas a la ___.
11. Para comprar cuadernos y lápices, puedes ir a una ___.
12. En esta tienda, puedes comprar rosas, tulipanes, plantas y muchas cosas más.

1. d **u** l c e r í a
2. a l m a c é **n**
3. c o m e s t i **b** l e s
4. s **u** p e r m e r c a d o
5. p a s t **e** l e r í a
6. p a **n** a d e r í a
7. l i b **r** e r í a
8. j o y **e** r í a
9. j u **g** u e t e r í a
10. z a p **a** t e r í a
11. p a p e **l** e r í a
12. f l **o** r e r í a

CAPÍTULO 9 Primer paso

Nombre ______________________ Clase ______________ Fecha ______________

**6a.** Adrián is new in town and needs your help in finding his way around. Answer Adrián's questions using the words in parentheses. Use expressions for giving directions you've learned like **al lado de**, **cerca de**, **lejos de** and **a dos cuadras**.

1. Café
2. Colegio
3. Florería
4. Correos
5. Almacén
6. Plaza de Armas
7. Hospital
8. Cine Bolívar
9. Parque Central
10. Gimnasio
11. Teatro Colón
12. Metro
13. Teléfonos
14. Garaje
15. Hotel San Martín
16. Zapatería
17. Policía
18. Pastelería
19. Juguetería
20. Tienda de comestibles
21. Casa de Julia
22. Casa de Adrián
23. Casa de Rafael
24. Casa de Enriqueta
25. Panadería

**MODELO** Perdón, ¿dónde está la zapatería? (la policía)
**La zapatería está al lado de la policía.**

1. ¿Me puede decir dónde queda el metro? (la Plaza de Armas)
   **El metro queda al lado de la Plaza de Armas.**

2. ¿Me puede decir dónde queda el colegio? (el almacén)
   **El colegio está a dos cuadras del almacén.**

3. Perdón, ¿dónde está la casa de Enriqueta? (la casa de Julia)
   **La casa de Enriqueta está a dos cuadras de la casa de Julia.**

**b.** Now Adrián thinks he knows his way around, but he still gets a little confused! Answer his questions with the correct information.

4. El café está cerca de la panadería, ¿verdad?
   **No, el café está lejos de la panadería.**

5. El Parque Central está muy lejos del hospital, ¿verdad?
   **No, el Parque Central está cerca del hospital.**

6. El gimnasio está a dos cuadras del Teatro Colón, ¿verdad?
   **No, el gimnasio está al lado del Teatro Colón.**

# SEGUNDO PASO

**7** **¡Qué desastre!** Your suitcase got lost on your flight from San Antonio to Cozumel, México, and now you have to fill out a lost baggage claim form. First fill out the top part of the form, then think of at least six articles of clothing you'd be likely to take on a week-long trip to Cozumel (a beach resort with plenty of archaelogical wonders nearby) and list them in the section of the form marked **Descripción del contenido**. Be sure to specify color and fabric, using the vocabulary on pp. 242 and 243 of your textbook.

| ***Hoja de reclamación—Irregularidad de equipaje*** | | | |
|---|---|---|---|
| *Nombre y apellido(s) del pasajero* | **Answers will vary.** | | |
| *Dirección permanente y teléfono* | | | |
| *No. de vuelo* 887 | *Mes* marzo | *Día* 14 | *De/A* San Antonio/Cozumel |
| *Descripción del contenido* | | | |

**8** Rufino is a new exchange student from Spain. In Spain, he often dresses up. He wants to know how he should dress in order to fit in with American students. Help him out by offering advice about what to wear in the following situations to be both comfortable and in style.

MODELO para ir a una fiesta
**Para ir a una fiesta no tienes que llevar ropa muy formal. Puedes llevar unos bluejeans y una camisa de algodón.**

1. para ir a una boda **Answers will vary. Possible answers:**
**Para ir a una boda debes llevar ropa bastante formal: un traje, una camisa blanca y unos zapatos de cuero.**

2. para hacer un picnic con unos amigos
**Para hacer un picnic con unos amigos debes llevar ropa bastante cómoda: unos bluejeans o pantalones cortos y una camiseta de algodón.**

3. para ir a clases en el invierno
**Para ir a clases en el invierno puedes llevar un suéter de lana o una chaqueta de cuero.**

4. para salir con una chica
**Para salir con una chica debes llevar ropa buena pero cómoda: una chaqueta con unos bluejeans o pantalones, una camisa blanca y unos zapatos o botas de cuero.**

5. para ir de compras
**Para ir de compras tienes que llevar ropa muy cómoda.**

6. para ir a la pizzería con unos amigos
**¡Para ir a la pizzería con unos amigos no debes llevar una camiseta blanca ni pantalones blancos!**

7. para ir a un partido de fútbol del colegio en el otoño
**Para ir a un partido de fútbol del colegio en el otoño debes llevar una camisa o chaqueta roja y amarilla. El rojo y el amarillo son los colores de nuestro colegio.**

**9** Can you come up with things that fit the following descriptions? You may use vocabulary from this chapter and earlier chapters. For additional vocabulary, see pp. 242–246 of your textbook.

MODELO algo más pequeño que una calculadora
**Unos aretes son más pequeños que una calculadora.**

1. algo más feo que una cucaracha *(cockroach)*
**Answers will vary.**

2. algo más grande que un elefante

3. algo más delgado que una serpiente

4. alguien más famoso que el presidente

5. algo más difícil que un examen de español

6. algo más caro que un coche nuevo

7. algo más barato que un disco compacto

8. algo menos de moda que los pantalones de cuadros

Nombre ______________________________ Clase ______________ Fecha ______________

**10** Christine is visiting San Antonio. Today she's shopping at El Mercado. She is shopping for gifts to give her family. First, complete Christine's questions by filling in the materials and patterns things are made of. Then, using the picture, help Christine decide what to buy by making comparisons between the things she mentions. In giving her your advice, consider price as well as what you think of each item.

**Answers will vary.**

1. ¿Qué le compro a mi papá, un cinturón, una cartera de **cuero** o una camisa?

______________________________

______________________________

2. Y para mi mamá, ¿cuál es mejor—el vestido o la bolsa?

______________________________

______________________________

3. ¿Qué le debo comprar a mi hermano Keith, un sombrero *(hat)* mexicano o un suéter de **lana**?

______________________________

______________________________

4. ¿Y a mi hermana Kelly, le compro el vestido de **algodón** o la blusa de **seda**?

______________________________

______________________________

5. ¿Qué le compro a mi hermano Doug, las sandalias o la chaqueta de **cuero**?

______________________________

______________________________

Nombre ____________________ Clase ____________ Fecha ____________

# TERCER PASO

**11** María and her friend Clara don't agree on much of anything. Read what María has to say about the following clothing items and then choose what you think her friend Clara would say.

__e__ 1. Esta falda roja es muy bonita, ¿no?

__d__ 2. Me encantan estos zapatos. ¿Te gustan?

__i__ 3. Esta chaqueta está de moda, ¿no crees?

__b__ 4. Cincuenta dólares por un cinturón. ¡Qué barato!

__a__ 5. Las botas negras son feas, ¿verdad?

__c__ 6. Este traje de baño no me queda muy bien.

__f__ 7. Ese suéter azul es de lana.

__h__ 8. Me gusta la falda de cuadros. ¿Cuál prefieres, la de rayas o la de cuadros?

__g__ 9. Los pantalones son muy largos.

a. No, son bonitas.
b. ¡Qué va! *(No way!)* ¡Es un robo!
c. No, te queda muy bien.
d. Bueno, yo prefiero esos negros.
e. No, es fea. No me gusta el rojo.
f. No, creo que es de algodón.
g. Pues, en realidad son bastante cortos.
h. La de rayas. Además, la otra no te queda bien.
i. Bueno, en realidad ya pasó *(it's out)* de moda. Además, es fea.

**12** Imagine that you're out shopping with a few friends at a thrift store. Each of them wants your advice about the clothes he or she is looking at. Answer their questions honestly!

1. 

Oye, ¿cuál de estas camisas prefieres? A mí me gusta la amarilla, y además, mira, ¡me queda perfectamente!

**Answers will vary.**

2. 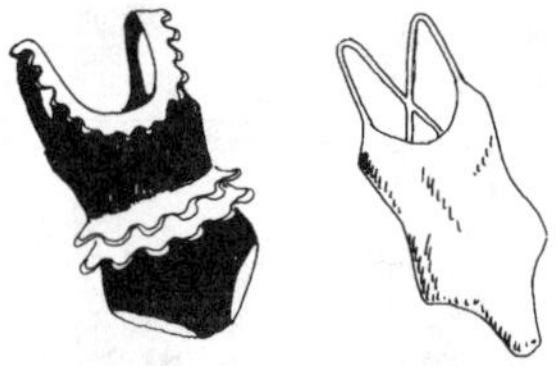

¿Qué traje de baño te gusta más? ¿El morado o el anaranjado? Es que me gustan los dos.

3. 

¿Cuáles de estos pantalones te gustan más? ¿Los verdes o los de cuadros?

4. 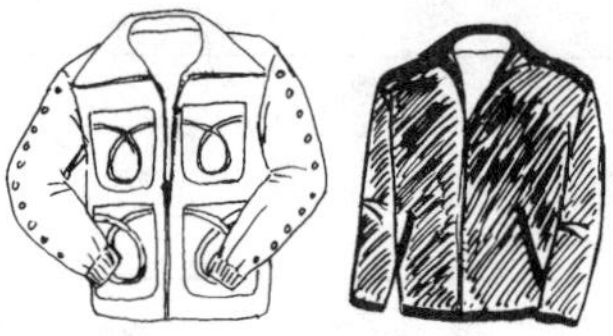

¿Qué chaqueta te gusta más? ¿Esta chaqueta gris o esa chaqueta parda?

**13** Below are some conversations between shoppers and store owners in El Mercado. Complete each conversation with demonstrative adjectives from the box.

| | | | |
|---|---|---|---|
| esas | esa | esos | este |
| estos | esta | ese | estas |

— Perdón, señor. ¿Cuánto cuesta **1.** __**este**__ *(this)* vestido? ¿Y qué precio tienen **2.** __**esos**__ *(those)* pendientes?

— **3.** __**Ese**__ *(That)* vestido cuesta $40.00. Y **4.** __**esos**__ *(those)* pendientes cuestan $28.00.

---

— Arturo, ¿ves **5.** __**esas**__ *(those)* camisetas allí? Me gustan mucho.

— ¿De veras? Prefiero **6.** __**estas**__ *(these)* camisetas aquí.

---

— **7.** __**Estas**__ *(These)* sandalias son menos caras que las otras de la otra tienda.

— Sí, pero **8.** __**esas**__ *(those)* sandalias de la otra tienda son más bonitas.

---

— Perdón, señorita... ¿Es **9.** __**este**__ *(this)* cinturón de cuero?

— Sí, joven. Todos **10.** __**esos**__ *(those)* cinturones allí son de cuero muy bonito.

— ¿Y **11.** __**estas**__ *(these)* carteras también?

— Sí, sí. Todo lo que vendemos aquí es de cuero... zapatos, sandalias, cinturones...

**14** The Estrada family is having a garage sale. Imagine you're at the sale, pointing things out to a friend. Look over the list of some of the things for sale. First tell your friend how much each thing costs and then comment on the price using the vocabulary on p. 248 of your textbook.

MODELO una blusa de seda por $4.00
**Esta blusa de seda cuesta $4.00. ¡Qué ganga!**

1. un estéreo viejo por $75.00
   **Answers will vary.**
   ______________________________________

2. una bicicleta para un chico por $12.00
   ______________________________________
   ______________________________________

3. 3 suéteres de lana por $10.00
   ______________________________________
   ______________________________________

4. unos juegos de mesa por $2.00 cada uno

5. 4 corbatas feas por $15.00

6. unos vestidos de algodón por $30.00 cada uno

**15** Imagine that you and a friend are shopping in a clothing store. You're looking for a new pair of pants and your friend is looking for a new shirt. You've narrowed it down to two pairs of pants, one white ($30) and one blue ($38), while your friend must choose between one brown shirt ($26) and one shirt with green stripes ($24). Using what you've learned in this **paso**, write a dialogue between you and your friend as you ask for and give each other advice on how your respective clothing choices look and how much they cost. Each of you should have at least four lines of dialogue.

**Answers will vary.**

# VAMOS A LEER

**16** Read this poem about a young girl named Maribel. Do you know anybody like her?

## La antojadiza

por Ángel Nieto Romero

Este es el cuento de la niña Maribel,
una antojadiza que todo quería tener.
Todo es verdad en este cuento°,
así todo pasó, no les miento°.

Siempre que a una tienda va,
con su mamá o con su papá,
a la buena niña Maribel
se le antoja todo lo que ve.

"Me gusta esto, me gusta eso,
y esto y eso y eso y aquello°,
y aquello y esto que hay acá°,
y eso y aquello más allá.

Papá, vamos, cómprame esto
mamá, por favor, quiero eso.
Mira eso, eso me gusta
y esto aquí no me disgusta.
Mira qué bonito. Lo necesito.
Lo quiero ahora, cuesta poquito°.

Me encanta eso, me encanta aquello,
eso me gusta, ¡Qué maravilla!
Esto es magnífico y eso también,
estoy segura° que me quedará bien.

Botas, sandalias, zapatos y
quiero hacerme unos retratos°.
Medias°, leotardos°, calcetines y
una familia de delfines°.

Mira qué lindo, mira qué bello°
quiero esto y eso y aquello,
ese pañuelo°, este sombrero°,
aquel vestido, ese plumero°,
esta camisa, aquellas gafas°,
la bicicleta, varias hamacas°,
una cama nueva y este sofá.
¡Cómpramelo todo, querido papá!

**cuento** *story;* **no les miento** *I'm not lying to you;* **aquello** *that;* **acá** *here;* **poquito** *a little;* **segura** *sure;* **retratos** *portraits;* **medias** *stockings;* **leotardos** *leotards;* **delfines** *dolphins;* **bello** *beautiful;* **pañuelo** *handkerchief;* **sombrero** *hat;* **plumero** *feather duster;* **gafas** *sunglasses;* **hamacas** *hammocks*

1. What do you think **antojadiza** means? **someone who wants everything they see**
2. In the line "se le antoja todo lo que ve," the phrase "se le antoja" could be substituted with
   **a.** tiene   (**b.** quiere)   **c.** necesita
3. How do you know Maribel likes the things she sees? What phrases does she use?
   **Me gusta esto; Mira qué bonito; Me encanta eso, me encanta aquello, ¡Qué maravilla! Esto es magnífico.**
4. What clothing items does she mention? **Botas, sandalias, zapatos, medias, leotardos, calcetines, pañuelo, sombrero, vestido, camisa, gafas**
5. Can you think of one item Maribel probably really doesn't need at all?
   **una familia de delfines/un plumero**

Nombre ______________________ Clase ____________ Fecha ____________

# CULTURA

**17** The following travelers are all in Miami International airport, heading to the following Spanish-speaking countries. What currency does each person or group need to get before their flights take off? Hint: Look over the maps on pp. xxi–xxvii of your textbook while doing this activity.

**dólares** 1. La familia Ybarra va a San Juan.

**pesos** 2. Daniel Benedetti va a Buenos Aires.

**pesos** 3. Adela Ramos va a Bogotá.

**sucres** 4. Beatriz y Felipe Malo van a Quito.

**pesetas** 5. Manolo Hurtado va a Madrid.

**colones** 6. Rafael, Karin y Esteban Fajardo van a San José.

**quetzales** 7. Irene Velásquez va a la Ciudad de Guatemala.

**pesos** 8. Humberto Carranza va al D.F.

**bolívares** 9. Anita Bermúdez va a Caracas.

**18** In the **Nota cultural** on p. 240 of your textbook you read about how people in Spain and many other Spanish-speaking countries often do their grocery shopping in specialty stores located in their neighborhoods. They usually buy just enough for one or two days at a time.

**a.** Now think about how people usually buy groceries where you live. Do they walk to shops near their homes? Do they buy just enough for a few days, or do they buy more?

**Answers will vary.**

**b.** The way you answered question **a.** depends on whether you live in a city or a suburb, a small town, or in the country. Would it be practical to go grocery shopping daily where you live? Why or why not?

**Answers will vary.**

Nombre ____________ Clase ____________ Fecha ____________

# Celebraciones



## DE ANTEMANO

**1** Everyone's talking while getting ready for a surprise birthday party for Yolanda. Match each of the questions and comments in the first column with the most appropriate response from the second column.

__f__ 1. A ver, ¿qué debemos escribir en el pastel?

__e__ 2. Oye, Diego. ¿Me ayudas a preparar los tamales?

__b__ 3. Rosa, ¿con quién estás hablando?

__d__ 4. Y tú, Chuy, ¿qué hiciste?

__a__ 5. ¿Sabes quién mandó las invitaciones?

__c__ 6. Aquí está el pastel. ¿Qué te parece?

**a.** Mario. También ayudó a comprar la comida.
**b.** Con Elena. Quiere saber qué necesita traer a la fiesta.
**c.** Perfecto. A Yolanda le va a encantar.
**d.** Pues, limpié la casa y después ayudé a preparar las decoraciones.
**e.** ¡Claro que sí! Me gustan muchísimo los tamales.
**f.** Pon "Feliz cumpleaños, Yolanda". ¿Qué más?

**2** Look at the **fotonovela**. What word or phrase would you use...?

1. to ask someone what they think of the decorations **¿Qué te parecen las decoraciones?**
2. to tell someone that you don't know and that he or she should ask María
   **No sé... pregúntale a María.**
3. to tell someone that you'll gladly do what he or she has asked you to do
   **¡Claro que sí!**
4. to ask someone what he or she did
   **¿Qué hiciste?**
5. to say that your sister prepared the food
   **Mi hermana preparó la comida.**
6. to say that you helped, too
   **Yo ayudé también.**
7. to say that you sent out the invitations
   **Mandé las invitaciones.**
8. to ask someone to help you buy the cake
   **¿Me ayudas a comprar el pastel?**
9. to say that you're talking to Beto
   **Estoy hablando con Beto.**

Nombre ____________ Clase ____________ Fecha ____________

# PRIMER PASO

**3** Fill in each calendar page below with the name of the holiday celebrated on that day in the U.S.

1. 14 de febrero — **Día de los Enamorados**
2. 4 de julio — **Día de la Independencia**
3. 1 de enero — **Año Nuevo**
4. 24 de diciembre — **Nochebuena**
5. 19 de junio — **Día del Padre**
6. 25 de diciembre — **Navidad**
7. 31 de diciembre — **Nochevieja**

**4** Every Sunday, Lupe's Tía Luisa calls from Guadalajara, wanting to know how everyone is and what everybody's doing. Using the cues below and following the model, answer Tía Luisa's questions.

MODELO TÍA LUISA ¿Está estudiando Inés? (leer el periódico)
LUPE **No, ahora está leyendo el periódico.**

1. ¿Y está lavando el carro Papá? (tomar una siesta)
**No, ahora está tomando una siesta.**

2. ¿Y Mamá? ¿Está trabajando en el jardín? (hablar con la tía Carmen)
**No, ahora está hablando con la tía Carmen.**

3. ¿Y está Ricardo escribiendo una composición *(composition)*? (leer las tiras cómicas)
**No, ahora está leyendo las tiras cómicas.**

4. ¿Están comiendo Sara y Martín? (salir para ir al cine)
**No, ahora están saliendo para ir al cine.**

5. ¿Y Lourdes? ¿Está corriendo en el parque? (limpiar su cuarto)
**No, ahora está limpiando su cuarto.**

6. ¿Y tú? ¿Estás preparando el almuerzo? (mirar la televisión)
**No, ahora estoy mirando la televisión.**

7. ¿Está Julia lavando los platos? (escuchar música en su cuarto)
**No, ahora está escuchando música en su cuarto.**

8. ¿Y están Toño y Susana lavando el carro? (jugar con sus juguetes)
**No, ahora están jugando con sus juguetes.**

**5** Every family celebrates holidays in a slightly different way. Pick one holiday you and your family celebrate, and describe what you and your family like to do on that day.

MODELO **Para el Día de Acción de Gracias, me gusta ir a visitar a mis tíos y primos... A mi hermano le gusta ver partidos de fútbol americano en la televisión.**

**Answers will vary.**

**6** **¡Pobre Ana!** She can't make it to her friend Paloma's party because she's sick, but she can't help calling Paloma to find out what's going on. Using the picture below as a guide, write Ana's questions and Paloma's answers. Number 1 is done for you as a model.

1. Bueno, Paloma, **¿qué estás haciendo?**
   **Estoy sirviendo las galletas en este momento.**
2. Y Rolando, está allí, ¿no? **¿Qué está haciendo?**
   **Está bailando y hablando con Beatriz.**
3. Hay música. **¿Quién está tocando la guitarra?**
   **Julio está tocando la guitarra y cantando.**
4. Y Miguel, está allí, ¿verdad? **¿Qué está haciendo?**
   **Sí, está aquí. Está escuchando a Julio.**
5. ¿Federico y Roberto? **¿Qué están haciendo?**
   **Federico y Roberto están comiendo, hablando y mirando la televisión.**
6. Y la comida, ¿ **crees que hay** bastante para todos?
   **Sí, creo que sí.**

**7** Describe where you are and what you are doing at each of the times below. Use the present progressive.

MODELO jueves—8:00 P.M.
**Estoy en casa. Estoy mirando mi programa de televisión favorito.**

1. lunes—7:00 A.M. **Answers will vary. Estoy desayunando en casa.**
2. jueves—12:30 P.M. **Estoy en la cafetería. Estoy hablando con mis amigos.**
3. sábado—8:00 A.M. **Estoy corriendo en el parque.**
4. viernes—9:30 P.M. **Estoy comiendo sándwiches con mis amigos en un restaurante.**
5. martes—4:00 P.M. **Estoy trabajando en...**

**8** Everyone is getting ready for a party. Use the expressions from the **Así se dice** box on p. 264 to create four short conversations between the people in the drawings about who to invite, what food to buy and prepare, and how to decorate the house.

MODELO — **¿Crees que debemos invitar al director del colegio?**
— **Sí, buena idea.**

**Answers will vary. Possible answers:**

1. 

— **¿Qué te parece si invitamos a toda la clase de español?**

— **Perfecto.**

2. 

— **¿Qué te parece si compramos más papitas?**

— **Sí, buena idea.**

3. 

— **¿Crees que hay suficiente (bastante) postre para todos?**

— **Creo que no. Necesitamos más galletas.**

4. 

— **¿Qué te parece si pongo los globos en la sala?**

— **Me parece bien.**

Nombre ______________________ Clase ____________ Fecha ____________



# SEGUNDO PASO

**9** Pedro's family is getting ready for a party. He's trying to avoid doing work, but without much success. Look at Pedro's responses under each picture and create a short conversation for each one in which Pedro either agrees or politely refuses to do what he's being asked to do.

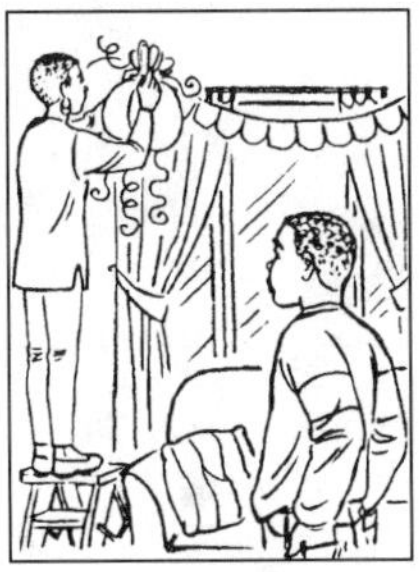

**1. sí**

**2. no**

**3. no**

**4. sí**

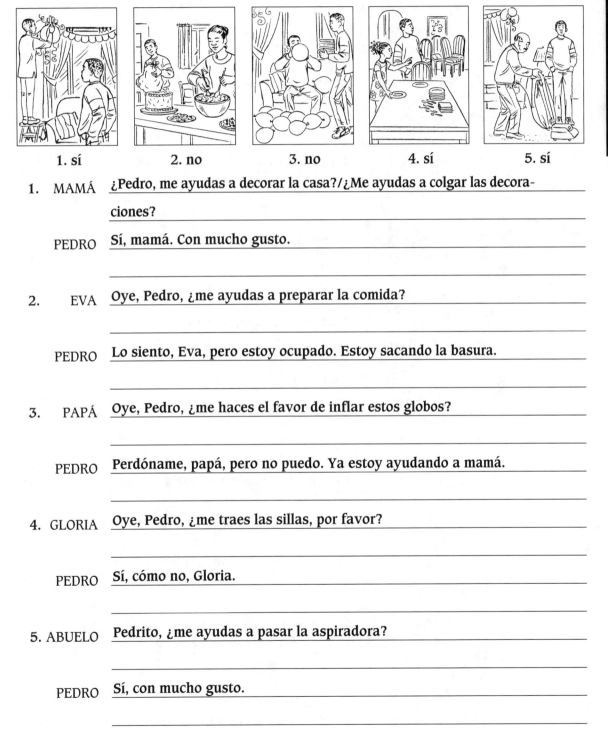

**5. sí**

1. MAMÁ **¿Pedro, me ayudas a decorar la casa?/¿Me ayudas a colgar las decoraciones?**

   PEDRO **Sí, mamá. Con mucho gusto.**

2. EVA **Oye, Pedro, ¿me ayudas a preparar la comida?**

   PEDRO **Lo siento, Eva, pero estoy ocupado. Estoy sacando la basura.**

3. PAPÁ **Oye, Pedro, ¿me haces el favor de inflar estos globos?**

   PEDRO **Perdóname, papá, pero no puedo. Ya estoy ayudando a mamá.**

4. GLORIA **Oye, Pedro, ¿me traes las sillas, por favor?**

   PEDRO **Sí, cómo no, Gloria.**

5. ABUELO **Pedrito, ¿me ayudas a pasar la aspiradora?**

   PEDRO **Sí, con mucho gusto.**

Nombre ______________________ Clase ____________ Fecha ____________

**10** Every summer all of Doña Engracia's grandchildren and some of their friends come to spend a couple of weeks with her at the beach. She makes sure things run smoothly by assigning chores to everyone. Write out Doña Engracia's instructions, using informal commands and what you see in each picture below.

MODELO 
Tomás
**Tomás, saca al perro y compra el periódico, por favor.**

1. 
Marta
**Marta, haz las camas, por favor.**

2. 
Blanca
**Blanca, organiza tu cuarto, por favor.**

3. 
Armando
**Armando, lava los platos, por favor.**

4. 
Teresa
**Teresa, lava la ropa, por favor.**

5. 
Guillermo
**Guillermo, pasa la aspiradora, por favor.**

6. 
Juan Pablo
**Juan Pablo, manda esta carta, por favor.**

7. 
Victoria
**Victoria, lava al perro, por favor.**

8. 
Paloma
**Paloma, lava el carro, por favor.**

9. 
Sergio y Mario
**Sergio, prepara el café, por favor; Mario, trae el pan.**

**11** Today it's your turn to wash the dishes and clean up the kitchen, but you need to start studying for your Spanish test tomorrow. Write a conversation between you and your brother or sister in which you explain the problem to him or her and ask for help. Your brother or sister should agree to help but should ask you to do a favor for him or her in return.

**Answers will vary. Possible answers:**

**—Gerardo, ¿me haces un favor?**

**—¿Qué quieres?**

**—Bueno... tengo un examen en la clase de español mañana. Necesito estudiar mucho, y...**

**—¿Y?**

**—¿Puedes lavar los platos y limpiar la cocina?**

**—Lo siento, pero...**

**—¡Por favor! El examen va a ser muy difícil.**

**—Bueno, de acuerdo. Pero ¿me ayudas a lavar el coche mañana?**

**—Claro que sí. ¡Gracias!**

**12** Imagine that you're "King or Queen for a Day" and have a chance to give the orders. Come up with six pieces of advice, recommendations, or instructions for your friends or members of your family, using informal commands of the verbs in parentheses and any other verbs you need.

MODELO (poner) **Para mi hermanito: Lava los platos y pon la mesa esta noche.**

1. (poner) **Answers will vary.**
2. (hacer) ______
3. (ir) ______
4. (venir) ______
5. (comprar) ______
6. (mandar) ______

Nombre ______________________ Clase ____________ Fecha ____________



# TERCER PASO

**13** Carla couldn't go to Consuelo's party last night, so she has called your sister to find out about it. Based on your sister's answers, write the questions Consuelo must be asking on the other end of the telephone line.

MODELO María Teresa preparó unas empanadas fantásticas.
**¿Qué preparó María Teresa?**

1. Miguel y yo llegamos a las 7:30.
   **¿Cuándo llegaron tú y Miguel a la fiesta?**
2. Susana llegó a las 8:00 y Marisa llegó a las 10:00.
   **¿A qué hora llegaron Susana y Marisa?**
3. Tomé muchos refrescos.
   **¿Qué tomaste?**
4. Salvador habló mucho con la chica nueva.
   **¿Qué hizo Salvador?**
5. María Luisa invitó a Juan a ir al cine.
   **¿Y María Luisa? ¿Qué hizo?**
6. Sí, todos bailamos mucho.
   **¿Bailaron mucho ustedes?**
7. Sí, todos lo pasamos muy bien.
   **¿Y lo pasaron bien todos ustedes?**
8. Terminó a las 11:00.
   **¿Cuándo terminó la fiesta?**
9. ¡Claro que sí! Ayudé a lavar los platos.
   **¿Ayudaste a limpiar después?**

**14** Ricardo wanted to get together with some friends yesterday, but no one was around. Looking at the pictures, tell what his friends did yesterday.

**1. Carlos y Javi**

**2. Sebastián**

**3. Marta, Luz y Ana**

**4. Gustavo y Andrés**

**5. Mis amigos y yo**

1. Carlos y Javi escucharon música.
2. Sebastián trabajó en el jardín.
3. Marta, Luz y Ana nadaron en la piscina.
4. Gustavo y Andrés montaron en bicicleta.
5. Mis amigos y yo estudiamos.

**15** Ana had ambitious plans for this week. In her list of things to do she's checked off the things she actually did and made some excuse for each thing that she didn't get around to doing. Using her list, complete the following conversation between Ana and her mother.

| |
|---|
| estudiar para el examen ✓ ¡3 HORAS! |
| mandar la carta a abuela ✓ |
| limpiar el cuarto llamó Gabi |
| caminar con el perro ✓ |
| ayudar a Juanito con la tarea ✓ ¡Sacó una A! |

1. MADRE Ana, ¿estudiaste para el examen de matemáticas?
   ANA **Claro que sí, estudié tres horas.**
2. MADRE Oye, Ana, ¿mandaste la carta a abuela?
   ANA **Sí, ya mandé la carta.**
3. MADRE Y limpiaste tu cuarto, ¿verdad mi amor?
   ANA **No, no limpié mi cuarto. Me llamó Gabi y hablamos mucho.**
4. MADRE **¿Caminaste con el perro?**
   ANA Sí, caminamos por todo el parque.
5. MADRE **¿Y ayudaste a Juanito con su tarea?**
   ANA Sí, ¿y sabes qué? ¡Sacó una A!

**16** You and Alfonso are planning the next Spanish Club festival. You've already made a list of assignments for the various tasks that need to be done. Use your list to respond to each of Alfonso's suggestions about who should do each task.

| | |
|---|---|
| dibujar el cartel | Laura |
| invitar a la directora | Alfonso |
| reservar el teatro | Susana |
| poner el anuncio en el periódico | Héctor |
| organizar el concierto | tú |
| escribir el programa | Nelson y Patricia |
| decorar el gimnasio | todos nosotros |
| tocar la guitarra | Isabel |
| preparar la cena | yo |

MODELO
ALFONSO ¿Quién va a dibujar el cartel?
TÚ **¿Qué te parece si Laura lo dibuja?**

1. ¿Quién va a tocar la guitarra?
   **¿Qué te parece si Isabel la toca?**
2. ¿Y quiénes van a decorar el gimnasio?
   **¿Qué te parece si todos nosotros lo decoramos?**

3. ¿Quiénes pueden escribir el programa?
**¿Qué te parece si Nelson y Patricia lo escriben?**

4. ¿Quién debe organizar el concierto?
**¿Qué te parece si tú lo organizas?**

5. ¿Quién va a poner el anuncio *(ad)* en el periódico?
**¿Qué te parece si Héctor lo pone?**

6. ¿Quién puede preparar la cena?
**¿Qué te parece si yo la preparo?**

7. ¿Quién va a invitar a la directora *(principal)*?
**¿Qué te parece si Alfonso la invita?**

8. ¿Quién debe reservar el teatro?
**¿Qué te parece si Susana lo reserva?**

**17** Everyone is preparing for the surprise birthday party for Alejandro. Answer the following questions using the preterite. Be sure to use the correct direct object pronoun (**lo, la, los,** or **las**).

MODELO ¿Quién llamó a Alejandro? (Sergio/anteayer)
**Sergio lo llamó anteayer.**

1. ¿Quiénes preparon la tortilla española? (Marcos y Graciela/anoche)
**Marcos y Graciela la preparon anoche.**

2. ¿Quién compró el helado? (Ricardo/ayer)
**Ricardo lo compró ayer.**

3. ¿Quién decoró la sala? (Herlinda y yo/anoche)
**Herlinda y yo la decoramos anoche.**

4. ¿Quién preparó las galletas? (yo/anteayer)
**Yo las preparé anteayer.**

5. ¿Quiénes compraron los refrescos? (Andrés y Rosario/la semana pasada)
**Andrés y Rosario los compraron la semana pasada.**

6. ¿Quién mandó las invitaciones? (Pilar/el sábado pasado)
**Pilar las mandó el sábado pasado.**

7. ¿Quiénes colgaron las decoraciones? (nosotros/ esta tarde)
**Nosotros las colgamos esta tarde.**

8. ¿Quién limpió la casa? (Anabel/ anoche)
**Anabel la limpió anoche.**

# VAMOS A LEER

**18** Each town and city in Spain has its own festivals and celebrations. These can be religious festivals or they can be celebrations commemorating a historical event. Other times, people celebrate just for the fun of it! That's the case of the celebration described below, called **La Tomatina**.

## La Tomatina:
## *Una fiesta colorida*

¿Te gusta el rojo? Pues, cada agosto, el pueblo° de Buñol, en el este de España, celebra una fiesta que se llama La Tomatina. Durante° esta fiesta, hay un color muy popular: ¡el rojo! Camiones° llenos° de tomates traen la carga a la plaza de Buñol y así empieza la fiesta de los tomates. En un solo día se tiran° unos 60.000 kilos de tomates sobre la gente de Buñol. No puedes esconderte° y si tienes buena puntería°, ¡mejor! Cuando la fiesta termina, todos van al río° para lavarse. Ahora, ¡a limpiar el pueblo!

**pueblo** *town*; **Durante** *During;* **camiones** *trucks*; **llenos de** *full of*; **se tiran** *people throw*; **esconderte** *hide*; **puntería** *aim*; **río** *river*; **alguien** *someone*

1. Why is this festival called **La Tomatina**?
   **People throw tomatoes at each other.**

2. Where does **La Tomatina** take place? Name the town and the country.
   **La Tomatina takes place in Buñol, in the eastern part of Spain.**

3. When is this celebration?
   **In August.**

4. How many tomatoes are used in the celebration? Over what period of time?
   **60,000 kilos of tomatoes are used; in one day**

5. How are the tomatoes transported to the town?
   **They're brought in by truck.**

6. Where do people go to clean up afterwards?
   **They go to the river.**

# CULTURA

**19** Saint's days, celebrated throughout the Spanish-speaking world, are associated with each day of the year. Special calendars called **santorales** show which saint is honored on that day. Children may be named for the saint on whose day they were born. For example, a boy born on April 3, the day of Saint Richard, could be named Ricardo. Below is the month of April taken from a **santoral**. Look it over, then answer the questions.

| DOM | LUN | MAR | MIER | JUE | VIER | SAB |
|---|---|---|---|---|---|---|
| | | | | 1 San Melitón | 2 Sta. Ofelia | 3 San Ricardo |
| 4 D. de Ramos | 5 Sta. Emilia | 6 San Celso | 7 San Donato | 8 Jueves Santo | 9 Viernes Santo | 10 Sábado Santo |
| 11 D. de Pascua | 12 San Damián | 13 San Hermenegildo | 14 San Valeriano | 15 Sta. Anastasia | 16 Sta. Engracia | 17 San Aniceto |
| 18 San Perfecto | 19 San Crescencio | 20 San Sulpicio | 21 San Anselmo | 22 San Sotero | 23 San Jorge | 24 San Alejandro |
| 25 San Marcos | 26 San Cleto | 27 Sta. Zita | 28 San Prudencio | 29 Sta. Catalina de S. | 30 Día del Niño | |

1. When in April will your friend Marcos celebrate his saint's day?
   **On the 25th of April.**

2. A couple had a baby girl in January and decided to name her Emilia after her grandmother. When will Emilia celebrate her saint's day?
   **On the 5th of April.**

3. If a baby boy is born on April 21, what might his parents choose to name him?
   **They might choose to name him Anselmo.**

4. One of your friends was born on April 23 and was named after the saint honored on that day. What is his name?
   **His name is Jorge.**

5. Your friend has a crush on a classmate of yours named Ofelia. When in April would be a good day for your friend to leave Ofelia a card in her locker? Why?
   **On the 2nd of April. Answers will vary.**

CAPÍTULO 11

Nombre ______ Clase ______ Fecha ______

# Para vivir bien

## DE ANTEMANO

**1** Match each of the following questions with the most appropriate response.

__d__ 1. Oye, ¿por qué no descansamos un poco aquí en esta banca?

__b__ 2. ¿Ustedes van al Museo Pablo Casals? ¡Yo también!

__a__ 3. ¿Tienes ganas de patinar sobre ruedas conmigo esta tarde?

__e__ 4. ¿Qué tal si vamos a la Plaza de Hostos esta mañana?

__c__ 5. ¿Adónde fueron hoy?

**a.** No, gracias. No quiero patinar porque no me siento muy bien.
**b.** ¿Sí? Entonces, ¿por qué no vas con nosotros?
**c.** Al Castillo del Morro. Debes ir allí también, porque es muy interesante.
**d.** ¡Buena idea! Estoy cansado y además me duelen mucho los pies.
**e.** Bueno, fuimos allí ayer. ¿Por qué no vamos a la Fortaleza?

**2** In the **fotonovela**, Ben, Carmen, and Pedro talk about where they went and what they did during their day in Old San Juan. Where have you gone lately? Complete the sentences below.

MODELO Anoche fui *(I went)* a...
**Anoche fui a la casa de mi amigo Greg para estudiar.**

1. El mes pasado fui a...
   **Answers will vary.**
2. El fin de semana pasado fui a...
   ______
3. Ayer después de clases fui a...
   ______
4. Anoche después de cenar fui a...
   ______
5. Esta mañana fui a...
   ______
6. Antes de la clase de español hoy, fui a...
   ______

# PRIMER PASO

**3** You're on your school's baseball team and tomorrow's the big championship game. Write sentences saying how each of the following people feel before the big game.

MODELO Yolanda/mal
**Yolanda se siente mal.**

1. Julio/cansado **Julio se siente cansado.**
2. Tú/muy bien **Tú te sientes muy bien.**
3. Ricardo/un poco mal **Ricardo se siente un poco mal.**
4. El entrenador *(coach)*/nervioso **El entrenador se siente nervioso.**
5. Yo/magnífico/a **Yo me siento magnífico/a.**
6. Alicia/muy confiada *(confident)* **Alicia se siente muy confiada.**



**4** For each situation below, say how each person feels. Use the words in the word box.

| | |
|---|---|
| **feliz** | *happy* |
| **triste** | *sad* |
| **horrible** | *awful* |
| **nervioso/a** | *nervous* |
| **enfermo/a** | *sick* |
| **enojado/a** | *upset* |
| **enamorado/a** | *in love* |

MODELO  **Alejandra se siente muy cansada.**

**Alejandra**

**Guillermo**

**Teresa**

**Mónica**

**José Luis y Margarita**

**Enrique y Paloma**

**Answers will vary. Possible answers:**

1. Guillermo **Se siente nervioso.**
2. Teresa **Se siente muy enferma.**
3. Mónica **Se siente enamorada.**
4. José Luis **Se siente feliz.**
   Margarita **Se siente triste.**
5. Enrique **Se siente bien.**
   Paloma **¡Se siente feliz!**

Nombre ______________________ Clase ____________ Fecha ____________

**5** Everyone's making plans for after school on the bus ride home. Can you match each invitation to its correct response?

1. <u>e</u>

¿Qué tal si patinamos sobre ruedas esta tarde?

a.

No, ya me siento bien. Sí, vamos... ¡quiero ver esa nueva película de aventuras!

2. <u>d</u>

¿Por qué no hacemos yoga en el gimnasio a las cuatro?

b.

Yo sí voy al partido, pero creo que Tomás no va a ir. Se siente mal hoy.

3. <u>a</u>

¿Quieres ir al cine esta tarde, o todavía te sientes mal?

c.

Nada, estoy bien. Nada más tengo que estirarme primero para no lastimarme los músculos.

4. <u>b</u>

¿Por qué no van Uds. al partido de béisbol conmigo?

d.

Hoy me siento un poco cansado. Tal vez podemos hacer yoga mañana.

5. <u>c</u>

¿Por qué no quieres levantar pesas conmigo? ¿Qué tienes?

e.

Gracias, pero no me siento bien hoy. No tengo ganas de patinar.

**6** Imagine that you're a fitness trainer and that you work in a sports club. What kind of suggestions would you give to each of the following clients based on what they tell you? Use the new vocabulary on p. 292 of your textbook, as well as sports vocabulary you learned in earlier chapters. In the box are some other possibilities. Use phrases like **¿Qué tal si . . . ?** and **¿Por qué no . . .?** to make suggestions.

| | |
|---|---|
| **el alpinismo** | *rock climbing/mountain climbing* |
| **las artes marciales** | *martial arts* |
| **el ciclismo** | *cycling* |
| **la equitación** | *horseback riding* |
| **el esquí acuático/alpino** | *water skiing/downhill skiing* |
| **el footing** | *jogging, running* |
| **el patinaje sobre hielo** | *ice skating* |
| **la tabla de vela** | *windsurfing* |

MODELO Me encanta estar en la playa. ¿Qué tipo de ejercicio puedo hacer?
**Bueno, ¿por qué no practicas el esquí acuático? Y también puedes hacer el footing.** **Answers will vary. Possible answers:**

1. Quiero practicar algún deporte, pero sólo me gustan los deportes solitarios.
**¿Por qué no haces yoga? También puedes levantar pesas.**

2. No me gusta el ejercicio, pero sí me gusta escuchar música.
**¿Por qué no haces ejercicios aeróbicos?**

3. Prefiero hacer ejercicio con otras personas.
**Pues, ¿por qué no juegas al tenis o al fútbol?**

4. No me gusta hacer ejercicio cuando hace calor. Prefiero el frío.
**Debes practicar el esquí alpino.**

5. No quiero ir a un gimnasio. Me gusta más estar en contacto con la naturaleza *(nature)*.
**Pues, ¿por qué no haces el alpinismo, el footing o el ciclismo?**

6. Prefiero hacer ejercicio adentro *(inside)*.
**¿Por qué no levantas pesas? O puedes hacer ejercicios aeróbicos.**

7. Tengo muchas presiones *(pressure)* y estrés en mi vida. ¿Cómo puedo llevar una vida más sana?
**¿Por qué no haces yoga? O puedes practicar las artes marciales.**

8. No me siento bien después de levantar pesas o correr.
**¿Qué tal si te estiras antes de hacer ejercicio?**

Nombre ______________________ Clase ______________ Fecha ______________

# SEGUNDO PASO

**7** Write a question asking each person or group pictured how she or he is feeling or what the matter is. Then write each person's answer to your question, using the expressions on p. 294 of your textbook and other words you know. Then explain why each person feels that way.

MODELO 

Begoña y Perla/una amiga estar enferma

**¿Porqué están preocupadas ustedes?**

**Estamos preocupadas porque una amiga está enferma.**

**Answers will vary. Possible answers:**

1. 

Blanca/hacer mal tiempo

¿ **Qué te pasa** ?

**Estoy enojada porque hace mal tiempo.**

2. 

Alonso/ser muy tarde

¿ **Tienes sueño** ?

**Sí, tengo sueño porque es muy tarde.**

3. 

Marcos/ya no tener fiebre

¿ **Cómo te sientes** ?

**Me siento mucho mejor, gracias. Ya no tengo fiebre.**

4. 

El señor Villalobos/no gustarle su cuarto

¿ **Está usted enojado** ?

**Sí, estoy muy enojado porque no me gusta mi cuarto.**

5. 

Begoña

¿ **Qué te pasa** ?

**Estoy enojada porque Ana no me invitó a su fiesta.**

6. 

Arturo/no saber nadar

¿ **Qué tienes** ?

**Tengo miedo porque no sé nadar.**

7. 

Francisco y Bernardo/montaña rusa *(rollercoaster)*

¿ **Por qué están nerviosos, Francisco y Bernardo** ?

**Estamos nerviosos porque no nos gustan las montañas rusas.**

8. 

Fernando y Celia/caminar mucho

¿ **Qué les pasa** ?

**Estamos cansados porque caminamos mucho hoy.**

Nombre ______________________ Clase ____________ Fecha ____________

**8** We all feel different emotions in various situations. For example, you might love the idea of going skydiving, while your best friend would be scared stiff. Complete the questionnaire below about how you feel in different situations.

MODELO Estoy feliz...
**Estoy feliz cuando salgo con mis amigos los viernes por la noche.**

Mis emociones

Estoy histérico(a) cuando... **Answers will vary.**

Me da asco° cuando como... ______________________

Estoy preocupado(a) cuando... ______________________

Estoy nervioso(a) cuando... ______________________

Estoy triste cuando... ______________________

Estoy feliz cuando... ______________________

**Me da asco.** *It grosses me out.*



**9** To test her biology class, Mrs. Robles gave her students this quiz on anatomy. Can you fill in the missing words from the drawing below? The first one is done for you as an example.

a. **el pelo**
b. **la cabeza**
c. **el/los ojo(s)**
d. **la/las oreja(s)**
e. **la nariz**
f. **la boca**
g. **el cuello**
h. **la garganta**
i. **el/los brazo(s)**
j. **la espalda**
k. **el estómago**
l. **el/los dedo(s)**
m. **la/las pierna(s)**
n. **el/los pie(s)**
o. **el/los dedo(s)**
p. **la/las mano/s**

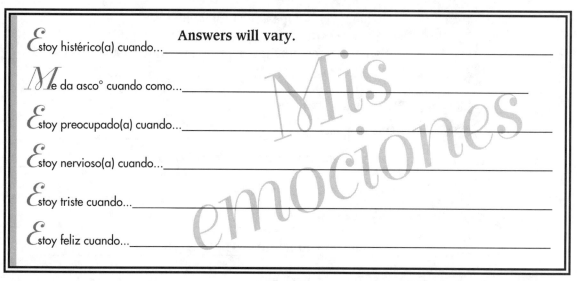

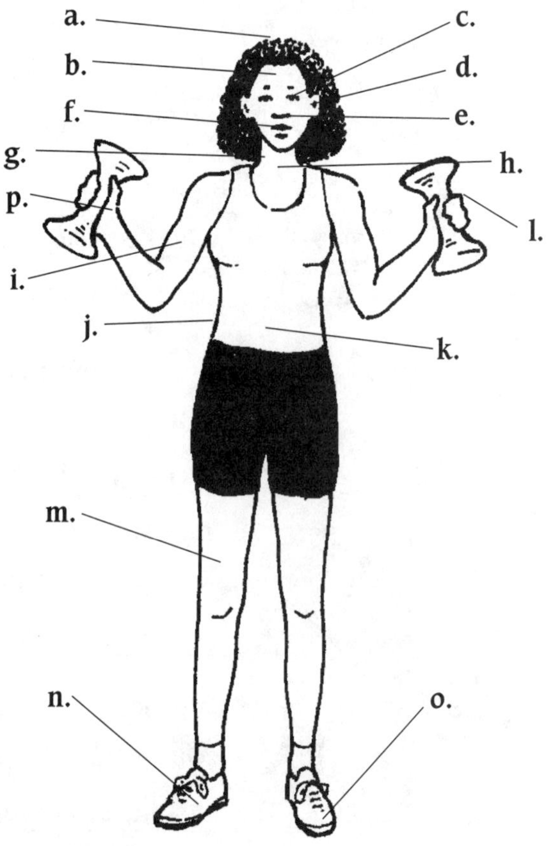

**10** Your school's hiking club just got back from a weekend excursion and a lot of people have minor aches and pains. Look at the drawings. Then describe what's wrong with each person and explain what he or she did or the condition that caused the problem.

jugar al fútbol · estar resfriado · levantar 20 kgs. · tener gripe · caminar sin zapatos · estirarse · comer mucha pizza · escribir por 3 horas

MODELO 
Claudia
**A Claudia le duelen los pies. Patinó sobre ruedas por muchas horas.**

1. 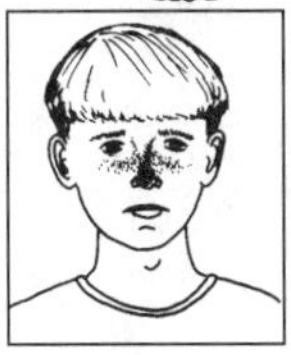
Sergio **Answers will vary. Possible answers: A Sergio le duele la nariz porque está resfriado.**

2. 
La profesora Aguilar
**A la profesora le duele la espalda. Levantó veinte kilos.**

3. 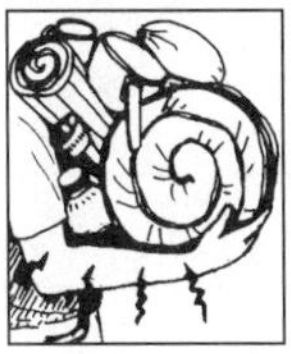
Tú
**A ti te duelen los brazos porque trabajaste mucho y no te estiraste.**

4. 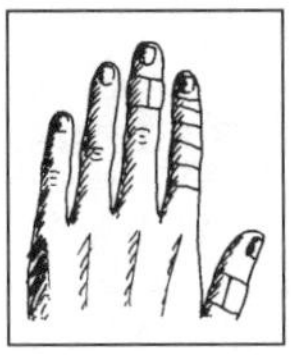
Elena
**A Elena le duelen los dedos. Escribió a máquina por tres horas.**

5. 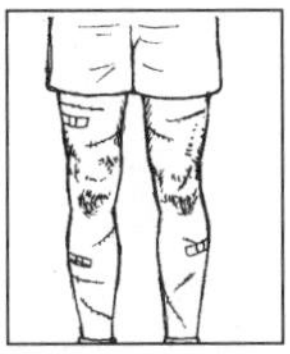
Daniel
**A Daniel le duelen las piernas. Jugó al fútbol toda la tarde.**

6. 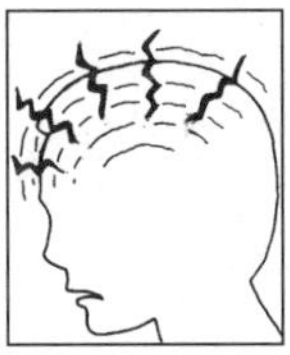
Yo
**A mí me duele la cabeza. Tengo gripe.**

7. 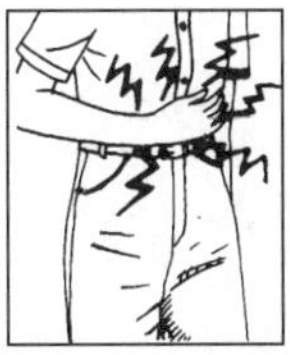
Laura
**A Laura le duele el estómago. Comió mucha pizza.**

8. 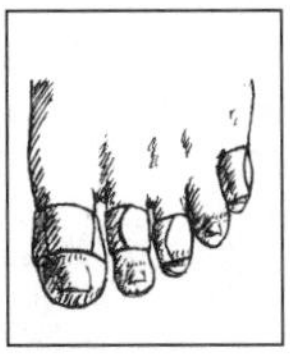
Miguel y Fátima
**A Miguel y a Fátima les duelen los dedos. Caminaron sin zapatos.**

Nombre ______________________ Clase ____________ Fecha ____________



# TERCER PASO

**11** Débora is trying to convince her friend Sebastián that most of their friends are athletic. What would Débora say to explain where each person or group of people went and what they did this last weekend, according to the pictures. Use the verbs **ir**, **jugar**, or other verbs in the preterite.

1. 
Débora (yo)
**Fui al parque y jugué al baloncesto.**

2. 
Sebastián (tú)
**Tú esquiaste.**

3. 
Tú y yo
**Tú y yo jugamos al voleibol.**

4. 
Carlos y Juanita
**Carlos y Juanita jugaron al tenis en la cancha de tenis.**

5. 
Rogelio e Iván
**Rogelio e Iván jugaron al béisbol.**

6. 
Diego y sus amigos
**Diego y sus amigos jugaron al fútbol en el estadio.**

7. 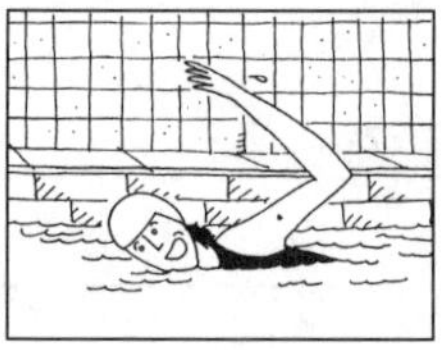
Patricia
**Patricia nadó en la piscina.**

8. 
César
**César fue al gimnasio y levantó pesas.**

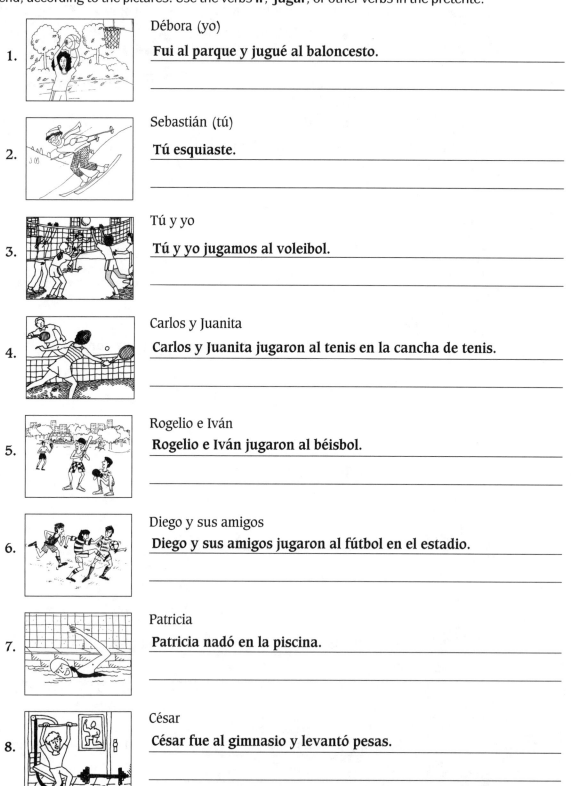

Nombre ______________________ Clase ____________ Fecha ____________

**12** When Sra. Castañeda gets home from work, she always wants to know where everyone went and what they did that day. Following the model below, write out Sra. Castañeda's questions and her son Nicolás's answers.

MODELO abuelo

SRA. CASTAÑEDA **¿Adónde fue abuelo?**

NICOLÁS **Fue a la panadería y compró unos panes dulces bastante ricos.**

1. tus hermanas

SRA. CASTAÑEDA **¿Adónde fueron tus hermanas?**

NICOLÁS **Fueron al cine y miraron una película.**

2. papá

SRA. CASTAÑEDA **¿Adónde fue papá?**

NICOLÁS **Fue al supermercado y compró comida.**

3. tú

SRA. CASTAÑEDA **¿Adónde fuiste?**

NICOLÁS **Fui a la piscina y nadé.**

4. Rodrigo y su amigo

SRA. CASTAÑEDA **¿Adónde fueron Rodrigo y su amigo?**

NICOLÁS **Fueron al gimnasio y levantaron pesas.**

5. el perro Sultán

SRA. CASTAÑEDA **¿Adónde fue Sultán?**

NICOLÁS **Possible answer: Fue al parque y caminó conmigo.**

CAPÍTULO 11 Tercer paso

**13** As you read in the **Sugerencia** on p. 302 of your textbook, using a Spanish-English dictionary can be tricky, especially when words have more than one meaning. For example, let's say you forgot how to say *tennis court*, so you look up *court* in the dictionary. But what do you find?

**a.** At first this listing may seem confusing, but by reading through it, you can figure out that Spanish translations of *court* are separated according to different meanings. For example, a *tennis court*, a *law court*, and a *royal court* all have different words in Spanish. What are they?

**la cancha, el tribunal, la corte**

If you read through the whole entry, you'll also see that *court* can be used as a noun or a verb in Spanish, just as in English. When you use a Spanish-English dictionary, make sure you know how you want to use the word and what part of speech it is. Otherwise, you might end up saying something pretty funny, like the person below!

**court** [ko:t] **1** *n* **(a)** (*Archit*) patio *m*; (*large room*) sala *f*.
**(b)** (*Sport*) pista *f*, cancha *f*; **hard** — pista *f* dura.
**(c)** (*royal*) corte *f*; **at** — en la corte; — **circular** noticiario m de la corte.
**(d) to pay** — **to** hacer la corte a.
**(e)** (*Law*) tribunal *m*, juzgado *m*; divorce — tribunal *m* de pleitos matrimoniales; **high** —, **supreme** — tribunal *m* supremo; **juvenile** — tribunal *m* tutelar de menores; **police** — tribunal *m* de policía; — **of appeal** tribunal *m* de casación; — **of inquiry** comisión *f* de investigación; — **of justice** tribunal *m* de justicia; **in open** — en pleno tribunal; **to laugh something out of** — rechazar algo poniéndolo en ridículo; **to rule something out of** — no admitir algo; **to settle out of** — arreglar una disputa de modo privado; **to take someone to** — demandar a uno; recurrir a la vía judicial.
**2** *vt woman* cortejar, hacer la corte a, (*less formally*) tener relaciones con; *favour* solicitar; *danger, trouble* buscar; *disaster* correr a.
**3** *vi* estar en relaciones, ser novios; **they've been —ing 3 years** llevan 3 años de relaciones; **are you —ing?** ¿tienes novio?; **—ing couple** pareja *f* de novios.

Excerpt from *Collins Spanish-English, English-Spanish Dictionary* by Colin Smith in collaboration with Manuel Bermejo Marcos and Eugenio Chang-Rodriguez. Copyright © 1971 by William Collins Sons & Co. Ltd. Reprinted by permission of ***HarperCollins Publishers Ltd.***

**b.** In a good Spanish-English dictionary, look up the following words: *play, back*, and *track*. Can you find different meanings and usages for each word?

***play***—**as a verb, jugar and tocar; as a noun, la comedia;** ***back***—**as a noun, la espalda; as a preposition atrás and detrás;** ***track***—**as a noun, huella (*animal track*), senda (*path, trail*), pista (*sports track*); as a verb, seguir or buscar.**

**14** Write a paragraph explaining several places where you and your friends and relatives went each day last week. What did each of you do there?

**Answers will vary.**



HRW material copyrighted under notice appearing earlier in this work.

# VAMOS A LEER

**15** Have you ever had mint tea to settle an upset stomach, or steaming hot lemon tea for a sore throat? Remedies such as these are very popular in the Spanish-speaking world. People suffering from mild ailments can buy mixtures of **plantas medicinales**, or *medicinal herbs*, at **yerberías**, open-air markets and pharmacies. The teas made from these herbs, called **infusiones**, are specially blended for different health problems.

Read through the descriptions of four **infusiones** below, then answer the questions.

**Laboratorios**
**Saluflor, S.A.**

Plantas medicinales **NATURA VITA**

NATURA VITA N° 5 DESCONGESTIVO RESPIRATORIO
Indicado en bronquitis, enfermedades pulmonares, resfriados y gripes. Tomada regularmente se evitan resfriados y aumenta las defensas del sistema respiratorio.

NATURA VITA N° 8 DIGESTIVO
Indicado en dolores de estómago, acidez y falta de apetito. Contribuye a mejorar la digestión.

NATURA VITA N° 11 CALMANTE Y TRANQUILIZANTE
Indicado en estados de estrés y ansiedad. Facilita un sueño natural y profundo. No crea dependencia.

NATURA VITA N° 13 ANTIRREUMATICA
Indicado en artritis, artrosis y problemas reumáticos en general.

Look at the words that appear in capital letters at the beginning of each description. Based on what you've read, which herbal tea do you think the pharmacy clerk might recommend to each of the following people?

**N° 11** 1. Mrs. Vasconcelos has a high-pressure job and can't seem to relax.

**N° 13** 2. Don Luis, 90 years old, is in pretty good shape, but when it rains his bones and joints ache.

**N° 8** 3. Mr. Guzmán sometimes eats too quickly and gets bad stomachaches.

**N° 5** 4. Luisa went outside without her raincoat on Tuesday and now she's got a cold.

# CULTURA

**16** **Yerba mate** is a tea that is enjoyed widely in South America. People typically drink **mate** through a metal straw, called a **bombilla**, from a hollowed-out gourd. Read the advertisement for **mate** below.

**EL MATE ES TU AMIGO FIEL**

La yerba mate es una extraordinaria bebida natural. Es como un amigo, un amigo fiel que comparte lo mejor de tu vida. Frío o caliente, éstos son algunos de los beneficios saludables de la yerba mate:

- ✔ *Es dietético.*
- ✔ *Vence al calor o al frío.*
- ✔ *Facilita la recuperación física.*
- ✔ *Mejora la digestión.*
- ✔ *Tiene un sabor rico.*
- ✔ *Disminuye el estrés.*

Which of the following benefits are claimed by the ad for **mate**? Check all that apply. Can you imagine any undesirable effects a stimulant tea might have?

1. __X__ helps you recuperate physically
2. ____ gives you energy
3. ____ helps with insomnia
4. __X__ tastes great
5. __X__ helps with digestive problems
6. __X__ lowers stress and tension
7. ____ helps with depression
8. __X__ helps you if you're dieting

**17** As you read in the **Nota cultural** on p. 298 of your textbook, baseball is popular in Caribbean countries. Besides following U.S. teams, these countries have formed leagues of their own. Along with the sport, Spanish has imported many baseball-related words from English, starting with **béisbol**. The headlines and captions below show how similar Spanish and English are when it comes to this sport.

**Canseco batea su 26to. jonrón del año**

**21er jonrón de Rafael Palmeiro**

**Lanza Hinojosa juego de un hit**

**Ponen out a Morelos en inning 11**

Look over the list of Spanish and English baseball vocabulary below. Can you match each Spanish word to its English equivalent?

__d__ 1. picheo
__e__ 2. ampáyer
__h__ 3. doble juego
__g__ 4. batear
__a__ 5. jonrón
__i__ 6. base
__c__ 7. liga
__f__ 8. doblete
__b__ 9. triplete

a. home run
b. triple
c. league
d. pitching
e. umpire
f. double
g. to bat
h. double-header
i. base

Nombre ______________________ Clase ______________ Fecha ______________

# Las vacaciones ideales

## DE ANTEMANO

**1** Imagine that you are touring Puerto Rico and have a free day in San Juan. Starting out at the **Plaza de Colón**, you figure that you have enough time to see five attractions before meeting up with friends at **El Morro**. Looking at the map of Old San Juan, write a postcard to your friends and suggest an itinerary, including five things you would like to see and do. Include the expressions **¿Por qué no...?** and **¿Qué tal si...?** in your suggestions.

MODELO **A mí me gustaría ver el Museo del Mar. ¿Por qué no vamos allí primero. Después, ¿qué tal si...? Y luego...**

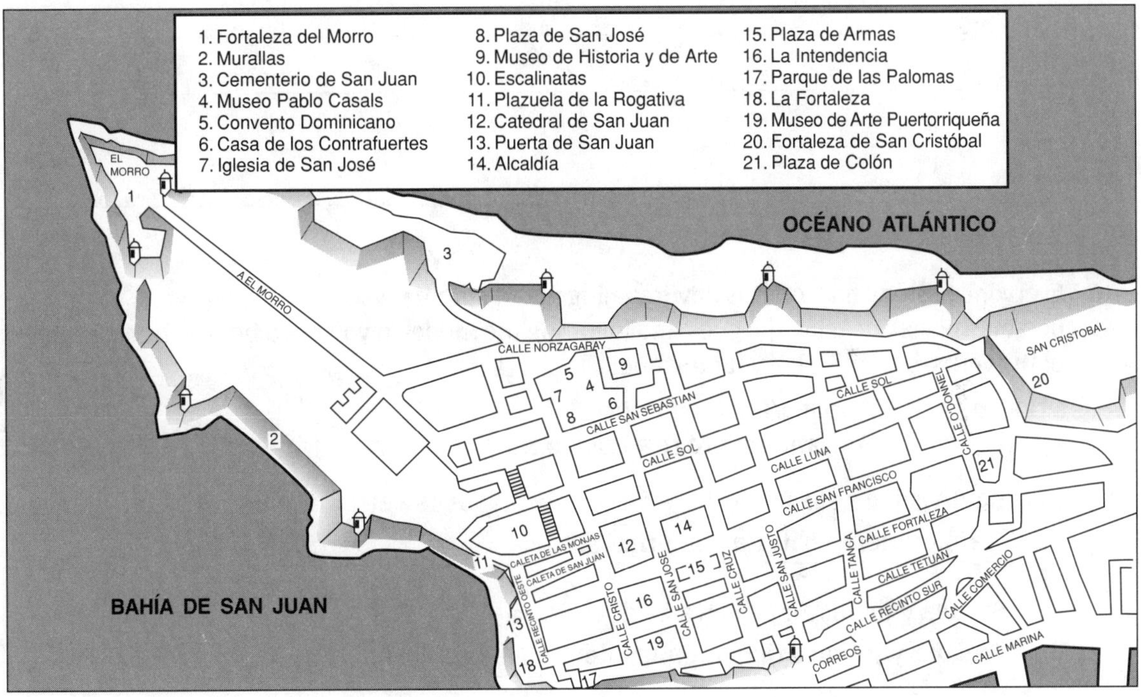


Answers will vary.

______________________________________________

______________________________________________

______________________________________________

______________________________________________

______________________________________________

______________________________________________

______________________________________________

Nombre ______________________ Clase ____________ Fecha ____________

# PRIMER PASO

**2** How much does your daily routine change when school's out? Make a list below of four things you do regularly during the school year. Then say how often you do them during the summer. Use the expressions from the box.

| | |
|---|---|
| muchas veces | a veces |
| nunca | todos los... |
| siempre | todos los días |

MODELO hacer la tarea
**Por lo general, hago la tarea casi todos los días. ¡Pero durante el verano, no la hago nunca!**

1. **Answers will vary.**
2. ______________________
3. ______________________
4. ______________________

**3** Everyone in study hall today is daydreaming about summer vacation. Explain what each person's plans are using the cues and following the model. If you need help with the forms of the verbs, see p. 318 of your textbook.

| | |
|---|---|
| preferir | (no) querer |
| (no) tener ganas de | |

MODELO Adriana/ir a Puerto Rico.
**Adriana quiere ir a Puerto Rico.**

**Answers will vary. Possible answers:**

1. Raúl/visitar a sus primos
**Raúl prefiere visitar a sus primos.**
2. Susana y Juanita/ir a Nueva York
**Susana y Juanita tienen ganas de ir a Nueva York.**
3. Yo/ir a California
**Yo quiero ir a California.**
4. La profesora/viajar a México
**La profesora tiene ganas de viajar a México.**
5. Isa y Ramón/ir a Miami
**Isa y Ramón quieren ir a Miami.**
6. Nosotros/descansar
**Nosotros tenemos ganas de descansar.**

**4** Everyone's going somewhere this summer! Write a question asking where the following people are planning to go, then write a response including what they'll do there. Use the expressions in the **Así se dice** box on p. 318 of your textbook, your imagination, and what you've learned about each destination.

MODELO Lourdes/San Antonio, Texas/primos/Paseo del Río
**Lourdes, ¿adónde vas a viajar este verano?**
**Voy a San Antonio. Allí quiero visitar a mis primos y ver el Paseo del Río.**

1. José Luis/Quito, Ecuador/montañas/mercado
**Answers may vary. José Luis, ¿adónde vas este verano? Voy al Ecuador. Quiero ver las montañas y visitar el mercado.**

2. Ernesto y Cristina/San Juan, Puerto Rico/El Yunque/El Morro
**Ernesto y Cristina, ¿adónde van ustedes?**
**Vamos a Puerto Rico. Allí esperamos ver El Yunque y El Morro.**

3. Óscar y yo/la Ciudad de México/las pirámides
**¿Adónde piensan ir tú y Óscar?**
**Óscar y yo vamos a ir a la Ciudad de México. Allí pensamos ver las pirámides.**

4. El director del colegio/Madrid, España/el Museo del Prado
**¿Adónde va a ir el director del colegio?**
**Va a ir a Madrid. Allí espera ir al Museo del Prado.**

5. Sara y Paloma/Miami, Florida/la Calle Ocho/la playa
**¿Adónde piensan viajar Sara y Paloma?**
**Van a ir a Miami. Allí piensan ir de compras en la Calle Ocho y descansar en la playa.**

**5** Now it's your turn to talk about summer plans. Write two sentences explaining what each of the people or groups of people listed below are planning for summer, using the expressions from the **Así se dice** box on p. 318 of your textbook.

MODELO mis primos
**Este verano, mis primos piensan hacer un viaje a Colorado. Van a estar allí por dos semanas.**

1. yo **Answers will vary.** ______
______

2. mis hermanos ______
______

3. mi mejor amigo/a ______
______

Nombre ______________________ Clase ____________ Fecha ____________

4. el/la profesor/a ______________________

______________________

5. mis compañeros de clase ______________________

______________________

6. mis vecinos *(neighbors)* ______________________

______________________

**6** Look at the pictures of the places that the people below are planning on going to for vacation. Write a sentence describing the weather there, then mention three things that each person or group of people will need to take with them, using the **Vocabulario** on p. 319 and other clothing vocabulary from Chapter 9. **Answers will vary. Possible answers:**

1. 

Herlinda

**Hace calor. Herlinda necesita llevar una cámara, unos pantalones cortos y un sombrero.**

2. 

Joaquín y Pilar

**Hace calor y mucho sol. Joaquín y Pilar necesitan llevar unos lentes de sol y un bloqueador.**

3. 

Luis y David

**Hace fresco y a veces llueve. Luis y David necesitan llevar unos suéteres, una cámara y unas chaquetas.**

4. 

La familia Dávila

**La familia Dávila necesita llevar mochilas, pantalones cortos y camisetas.**

5. 

María

**Hace mucho frío y a veces nieva. María necesita llevar una bufanda, una chaqueta y unos esquís.**

6. 

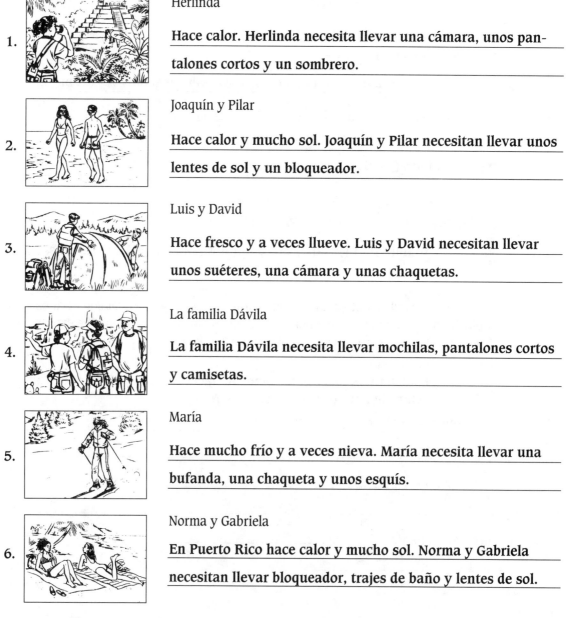

Norma y Gabriela

**En Puerto Rico hace calor y mucho sol. Norma y Gabriela necesitan llevar bloqueador, trajes de baño y lentes de sol.**

Nombre ______________________ Clase ____________ Fecha ____________

# SEGUNDO PASO

**7** One night at dinner, Raquel and her family began talking about their dream vacations. Complete Raquel's description of her family's opinions using the new words on p. 322 of your textbook. Do her family's ideas of the perfect vacation sound like yours?

¿Cuáles son nuestras vacaciones ideales? Pues... depende de la persona. A mí me gustaría 1. **bajar** el río Colorado en 2. **canoa** y ver el Gran Cañón desde el río. A mi hermano le gustaría 3. **explorar** la selva tropical del Brasil. Mi padre prefiere 4. **ir de vela**. Pero a mi madre le encanta la idea de 5. **hacer turismo** en todas las grandes ciudades europeas, como Madrid, París y Londres. ¿Y mis abuelos? Pues, a mi abuela le gustaría 6. **escalar** las montañas en Colorado. Por su parte, mi abuelo prefiere 7. **acampar/caminar** en el Parque Nacional de Yellowstone.

**8** Everyone's studying for the final exam in Spanish, but they all take a few minutes to think about what they'd rather be doing! Write a question asking Damián what he and his friends would like to do. Then in Items 1–5, write the answers Damián would give about himself and each of his friends.

**1. Damián** **2. Silvia** **3. Eugenio** **4. Rosa** **5. Maricarmen**

Pregunta: **¿Qué les gustaría hacer a ti y a tus amigos?**

1. **A mí me gustaría tomar el sol en la playa.**
2. **A Silvia le gustaría caminar en un parque nacional con su perro.**
3. **Eugenio tiene ganas de saltar en paracaídas.**
4. **Rosa tiene ganas de bajar un río en canoa con una amiga.**
5. **A Maricarmen le gustaría ir de vela.**

**9** Look over the **Gramática** section on p. 325. Would you use **ser** or **estar** in each of the situations below? Explain which verb you would use and why.

1. to ask your mom where your jacket is **estar—location**
2. to ask a friend why he or she's so upset **estar—state or condition**
3. to tell someone on the bus the time **ser—time**
4. to describe your little brother or sister **ser—description**
5. to find out who the person at your friend's party is **ser—definition/identity**
6. to tell your teacher where your homework is **estar—location**
7. to describe the great sweater your parents got you for your birthday **ser—material**
8. to tell the doctor how you are feeling **estar—state or condition**

**10** Lupe is at the beach writing a letter to her cousin Jesús back home in San Antonio. Complete the letter with the correct form of **ser** or **estar**. If you need help deciding which verb to use, look over the **Gramática** box on p. 325 of your textbook.

*Querido Jesús,*

*¡Saludos desde la playa! Aquí* **1.** **estoy** *(yo) en Puerto Dorado. ¡Este lugar* **2.** **es** *increíble! La playa* **3.** **es** *muy bonita y grande.*

*No* **4.** **estamos** *(nosotros) aburridos para nada, porque hay muchísimas cosas que hacer. Por ejemplo, hoy Sara y José* **5.** **están** *aprendiendo° a saltar en paracaídas. Y yo* **6.** **estoy** *tomando clases de tabla vela°.*

*Hay unos muchachos aquí que también* **7.** **son** *de San Antonio.* **8.** **Son** *muy simpáticos, y todos vamos a salir esta noche a bailar.*

*Ahora* **9.** **son** *las doce y media. Hace sol y calor. A la una, vamos a almorzar en un café que* **10.** **está** *muy cerca de nuestro hotel. La comida aquí* **11.** **es** *riquísima.*

*Bueno, es todo por ahora.* **12.** **Estoy** *(yo) un poco cansada porque caminé con Sara esta mañana por la playa. ¡Caminamos cuatro millas y ahora me duelen las piernas!*

*Espero que estés bien. ¡Saludos a todos!*

*Un beso,*

*Lupe*

**aprendiendo** *learning* **tabla vela** *windsurfing*

**11** Diana and Gustavo have one more test to go before vacation begins. Write out a dialogue between them based on the cues below. If you're unsure of whether to use **ser** or **estar**, refer to p. 325 of your textbook.

| Diana | Gustavo |
| --- | --- |
| Asks Gustavo how he's doing.<br>**Hola, Gustavo. ¿Cómo estás?** | Says he's a little tired, because he studied a lot last night.<br>**Hola, Diana. Estoy un poco cansado porque estudié mucho anoche.** |
| Says that she's nervous because she has a test.<br>**Estoy nerviosa porque tengo un examen.** | Says he is, too. Asks Diana if she packed her suitcase last night.<br>**Yo también. Oye, ¿hiciste la maleta anoche?** |
| Says she packed it at 11:00. Asks Gustavo if he already bought his ticket.<br>**La hice a las once. ¿Ya compraste tu boleto?** | Says he hasn't bought it yet.<br>**No, todavía no.** |
| Says she feels like leaving right now.<br>**Tengo ganas de salir ahora.** | Says he feels nervous. Says he also feels like leaving now.<br>**Yo estoy nervioso. También tengo ganas de salir ahora.** |

**12** You and a group of friends are trying to plan a trip this summer. Everyone has a different idea about where to go and what to do. Choose your favorite activity from those on p. 322 of your textbook (or another activity you like) and try to convince your friends to join you. Write a short paragraph explaining where you want to go, what you want to do, and why.

MODELO **Creo que debemos ir al Parque Yosemite para acampar porque...**

**Answers will vary.**

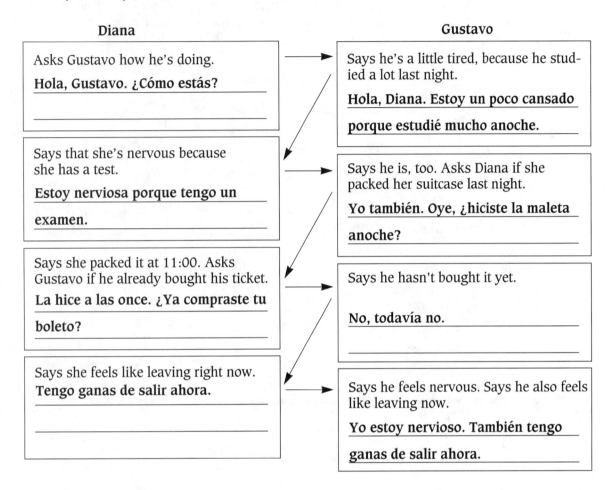

# TERCER PASO

**13** Below is a postcard from Carmen to one of her friends in New York. Complete the postcard using the correct preterite forms of the verbs in parentheses. If you need help with the preterite verb forms, see p. 327 of your textbook.

*Querida Tamara,*

*¡Hola! Nosotros* **1.** *(llegar)* **llegamos** *a Puerto Rico la semana pasada y lo estamos pasando muy bien. El fin de semana pasado Ben y yo* **2.** *(ir)* **fuimos** *a la capital e* **3.** *(hacer)* **hicimos** *un recorrido por el Viejo San Juan. Nosotros* **4.** *(visitar)* **visitamos** *el Museo Casals y El Morro. Yo* **5.** *(comprar)* **compré** *unos regalos también. ¡Nosotros* **6.** *(caminar)* **caminamos** *mucho ese día! Ayer mamá nos* **7.** *(llevar)* **llevó** *al bosque tropical, El Yunque. ¡Es increíble! Allí yo* **8.** *(escalar)* **escalé** *una montaña con Ben y nosotros* **9.** *(explorar)* **exploramos** *el bosque. Mamá* **10.** *(sacar)* **sacó** *muchas fotos de nosotros. Y esta tarde* **11.** *(jugar)* **jugué** *al béisbol con mi tío y mis primos. Bueno, me despido. Nos vemos pronto.*

*Un beso,*

*Carmen*

*Tamara Santander*
*623 W. 125th St., # 3B*
*New York, NY 10012*

**14** Now it's your turn. Write a postcard to a friend or relative and tell him or her what you did on vacation. You can describe your last real vacation or make up details about an imaginary one. If you need help with the preterite verb forms, see p. 327 of your textbook.

**Answers will vary.**

Nombre ____________________ Clase ____________ Fecha ____________

**15** Where did the following people go last summer? What did they do? Use the art and the cues provided to write complete answers.

**Answers will vary. Possible answers:**

1. 

Ellos/hacer un viaje a Costa Rica/escalar montañas/explorar la selva

**Ellos hicieron un viaje a Costa Rica. Allí escalaron montañas y exploraron la selva.**

2. 

Tus amigos/ir a Puerto Rico/visitar el Viejo San Juan

**Esteban, Emilia y Rogelio fueron a Puerto Rico. Allí visitaron el Viejo San Juan.**

3. 

Arturo/ir a ninguna parte/tomar una clase de francés/estudiar mucho

**Arturo no fue a ninguna parte. Tomó una clase de francés y estudió mucho.**

4. 

Tus primos/acampar en un parque nacional/caminar por el bosque

**Mis primos acamparon en un parque nacional. Allí caminaron por el bosque.**

5. 

Diego y Guillermo/ir al lago/pescar/nadar

**Diego y Guillermo fueron al lago con sus padres. Allí pescaron y nadaron.**

6. 

Sonia y Rubén/ir a México/explorar ruinas

**Sonia y Rubén fueron a México. Allí exploraron las ruinas.**

7. 

Los Alvarado/ir a España/visitar catedrales y museos

**Los Alvarado fueron a España. Allí visitaron muchas catedrales y museos.**

**16** There's been a computer problem at the travel agency, and now the plane tickets have gotten mixed up. Help sort out the tickets. Read what each person says about his or her trip and figure out which ticket belongs to him or her. Write the person's name on the right ticket.

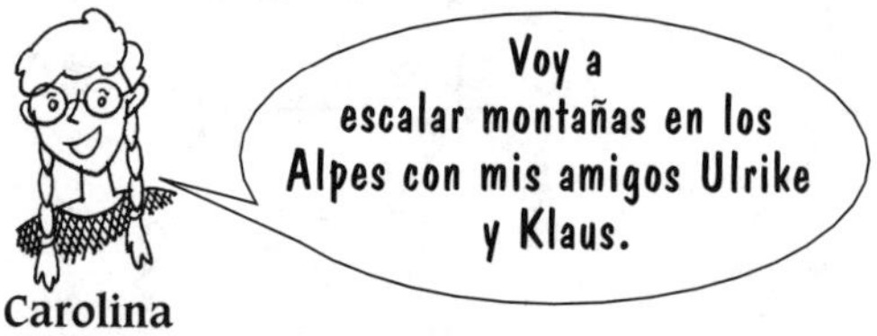

Voy a escalar montañas en los Alpes con mis amigos Ulrike y Klaus.

Carolina

Soy profesor de arqueología. Voy a investigar las pirámides.

El profesor Valdés

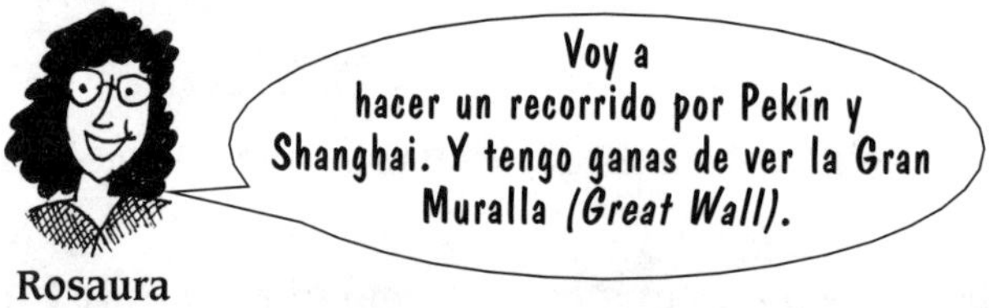

Voy a hacer un recorrido por Pekín y Shanghai. Y tengo ganas de ver la Gran Muralla *(Great Wall)*.

Rosaura

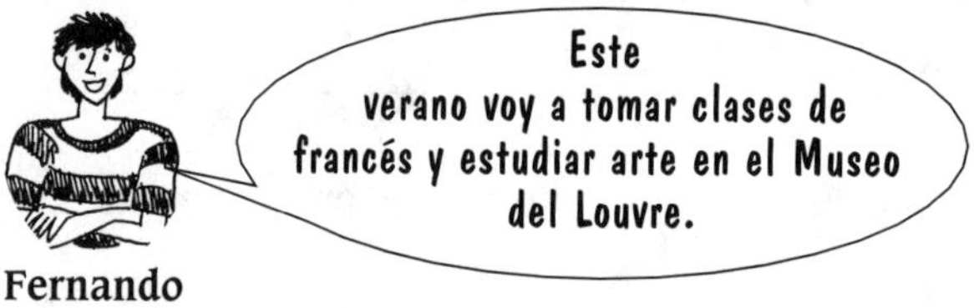

Este verano voy a tomar clases de francés y estudiar arte en el Museo del Louvre.

Fernando

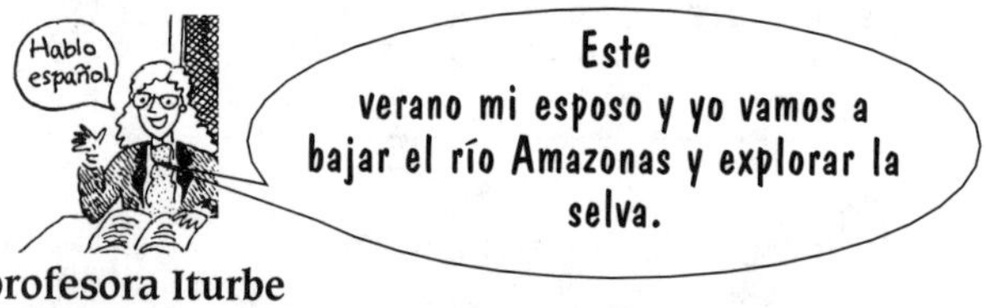

Hablo español
Este verano mi esposo y yo vamos a bajar el río Amazonas y explorar la selva.

La profesora Iturbe

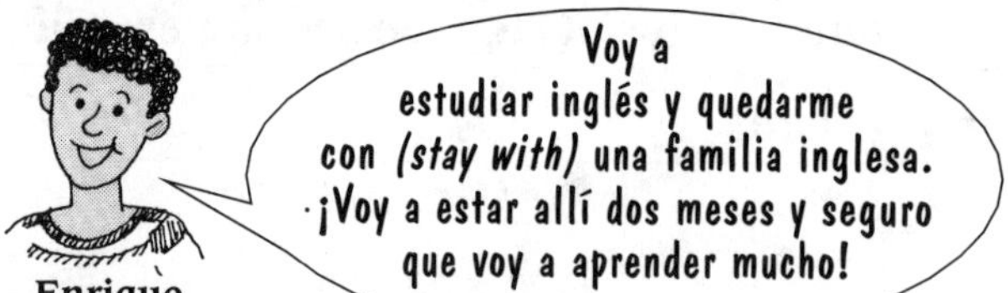

Voy a estudiar inglés y quedarme con *(stay with)* una familia inglesa. ¡Voy a estar allí dos meses y seguro que voy a aprender mucho!

Enrique

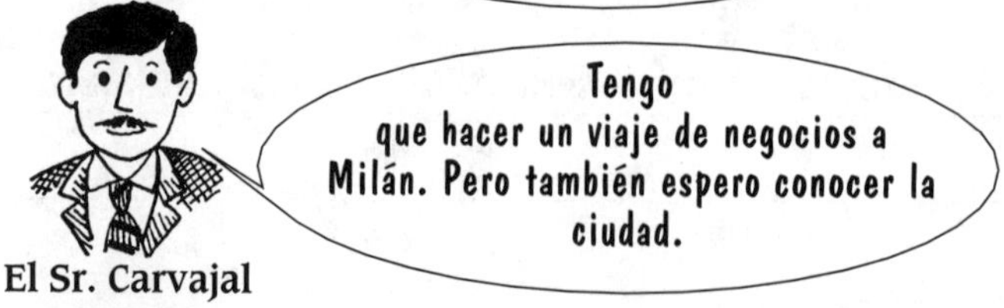

Tengo que hacer un viaje de negocios a Milán. Pero también espero conocer la ciudad.

El Sr. Carvajal

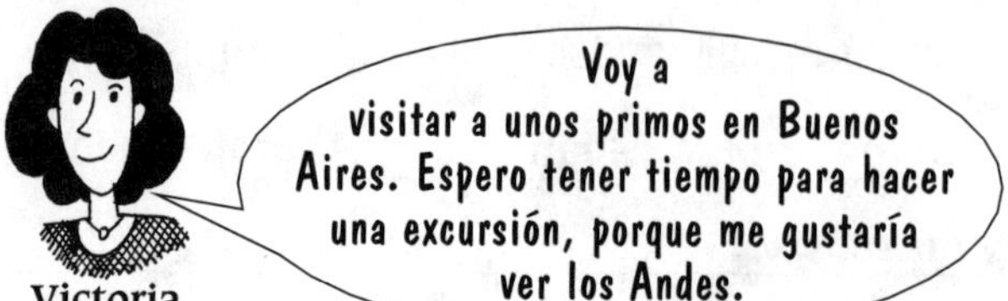

Voy a visitar a unos primos en Buenos Aires. Espero tener tiempo para hacer una excursión, porque me gustaría ver los Andes.

Victoria

**Nombre:** Enrique
**Destino:** Inglaterra

**Nombre:** Victoria
**Destino:** Argentina

**Nombre:** Carolina
**Destino:** Alemania

**Nombre:** ____________
**Destino:** Costa Rica

**Nombre:** El Sr. Carvajal
**Destino:** Italia

**Nombre:** Rosaura
**Destino:** China

**Nombre:** El profesor Valdés
**Destino:** Egipto

**Nombre:** Fernando
**Destino:** Francia

**Nombre:** La profesora Iturbe
**Destino:** Brasil

Nombre ______________________ Clase ____________ Fecha ____________

# VAMOS A LEER

**17** Below is a brochure describing a summer camp program in Spain. Look over the brochure, then answer the questions.

## Campamento de verano
**San Martín del Pinar** ***desde 1978***

**Lugar** Campamento San Martín del Pinar, ubicado cerca de Jaca (Huesca), al pie de los Pirineos. Nuestro campamento cuenta con comedor cubierto, enfermería, servicios y duchas de agua caliente y fría, piscina, canchas de tenis y de fútbol, pista de correr, picadero de caballos y un río donde realizar diversas actividades acuáticas.

**Fecha** 10 de julio al 30 de agosto.

**Participantes** Niños y jóvenes entre los 8 y los 16 años.

**Metodología**
- Actividades según grupos de edad.
- Hay un monitor por cada 10 participantes.
- Responsables jóvenes monitores, con formación en educación física, artes y sicología.
- Programa y entrenamiento reconocidos por las Comunidades Autónomas.

**Actividades**
Gran variedad de actividades deportivas y recreativas, natación, equitación, tiro con arco, fuegos de campamento, excursiones y marchas, clases de inglés con monitores norteamericanos y mucho más.

**Importe** 56.000 Ptas. por dos semanas

**El importe incluye...**
Transporte en autobús desde Barcelona y regreso, comida, desayuno, merienda, cena, alojamiento en tiendas, material de actividades, supervisión continua de monitores, transporte durante las excursiones y servicios de enfermería.

**Plazo de inscripción** Hasta el 20 de junio

**Para mayor información**
Viajes Euro-Ibéricos, S.A.
C/. Leñeros, 61
34022 Madrid
O llame al **(91) 556 78 43/77 21**

1. Where is the camp located? What are three things the brochure mentions about the place?
**Near Jaca, Huesca. Answers will vary: it has a pool, it's near a river, it has showers with hot and cold water, there are horses, it has a health facility.**

2. What is the age group of the campers? **From 8-16 years old.**

3. Look over the activities offered. You should recognize some of the words in this section. Can you use context and cognates to guess the meaning of the following? Match each word with its English equivalent.

| | | |
|---|---|---|
| **c** | 1. monitores | a. *hikes* |
| **d** | 2. equitación | b. *archery* |
| **e** | 3. fuegos de campamento | c. *instructors/counselors* |
| **a** | 4. marchas | d. *horseback riding* |
| **b** | 5. tiro con arco | e. *campfires* |

4. If you could go to the perfect summer camp, where would it be and what would you do? Write a description of the ideal summer camp, using the brochure above as a model. Include details about location, campers, activities, sports, and recreation.
**Answers will vary.**

Nombre ______________________ Clase ____________ Fecha ____________

# CULTURA

**18** In many parts of the Spanish-speaking world, students go on **excursiones de fin de curso**. Students begin saving money for the trip well in advance, and often have fund-raising activities to help cover costs. Imagine that you are an exchange student in one of the Spanish-speaking countries you have learned about this year. Use what you know about that country's history, culture, and geography to write a paragraph explaining where you think the class should go on its **excursión**. Say what you and your classmates could see and do in that place, and mention aspects like weather and cost to help convince the class.

**Answers will vary.**

**19** In the **Nota cultural** on p. 326 you read about the historic **paradores**. Spending the night at a **parador** can be fun, but it's not cheap. If you're traveling on a budget, there are cheaper possibilities. In Spain, your choices range from higher-priced **hoteles** to moderate **hostales** *(hostels* or *inns)*, or from inexpensive **pensiones** to **casas de huéspedes** *(boarding houses)*. All of these accommodations are rated with a set number of stars, according to what comforts they offer. So, you don't need to stay at a **parador** to be comfortable. Look over the advertisement for the Hotel "Cantabria". Then correct the statements that follow if they are false.

> *Hotel "Cantabria"* ★★
>
> Sólo un hotel ubicado en las montañas puede ofrecerle todas las comodidades para que descanse tranquilo. Aquí hay más de 30 habitaciones; todos con baño completo; televisión en color; teléfono.
>
> Salones para cursos y convenciones.
>
> Platos típicos.
>
> "Cantabria"; el nombre mismo invita al descanso, al disfrute de la naturaleza. El terreno verde presenta posibilidades de ocio por todo el año.
>
> - Excursiones de montaña.
> - Deportes acuáticos.
> - Deportes de invierno.
> - Escalada.
> - Parapente
> - Ala delta.
>
> O, si lo prefiere, descanso absoluto.

1. The Hotel "Cantabria" is in the mountains.
   **True.**
2. The hotel is very small, with only about 10 rooms.
   **False, it's rather large, with more than 30 rooms.**
3. The hotel serves food.
   **True.**
4. The rooms don't have televisions.
   **False. All rooms have a color television.**
5. The hotel is only open in the summer.
   **False. The ad mentions year-round outdoor activities.**

Nombre ______________________ Clase ____________ Fecha ____________



# EN MI CUADERNO

Describe an ideal friend, telling what he or she likes or dislikes. Include his or her age, where he or she is from, and some activities he or she likes.

Nombre ______________________ Clase ____________ Fecha ____________

# EN MI CUADERNO

Next Monday is the first day of school. This weekend, you're going shopping. Write about what you already have and what you still need for school. You might want to include some other things you're thinking of buying for yourself.

Nombre ______________________ Clase ____________ Fecha ____________

# EN MI CUADERNO

Write a letter describing yourself to a potential cabin mate at summer camp. Give your name and age. Describe both your physical traits and your personality. Incude in your description an activity or two you like or don't like at school. Then ask for your potential cabin mate's age, personality, and likes and dislikes.

CAPÍTULO 3 En mi cuaderno

Nombre ______________________ Clase ______________ Fecha ______________

# EN MI CUADERNO

You're making plans with a friend for next weekend. Create a conversation in which the two of you decide on the days, times, and activities you'll be doing, where you'll be going, and with whom.

Nombre ______________ Clase ______________ Fecha ______________

# EN MI CUADERNO

Tell a pen pal what each season is like where you live and what activities you like to do with your friends during each of them. Then ask your pen pal what the climate is like where he or she lives.

# EN MI CUADERNO

Describe your favorite relative. Write about his or her personality traits and what you enjoy doing together. Use an imaginary relative if you wish.

Nombre ______________________ Clase ____________ Fecha ____________



# EN MI CUADERNO

Tell the story of an ideal day from morning to evening. Tell what you plan to do, where you're going to go, when, and with whom.

# EN MI CUADERNO

Write a conversation in which you order your ideal meal at your favorite restaurant. Tell the server why you like to go to this restaurant. As part of your conversation, ask the server how much the bill is and determine if you need to leave a tip on the table.

Nombre ____________ Clase ____________ Fecha ____________

# EN MI CUADERNO

Imagine that you've been in an accident and are going to be home for a week. Your friends and neighbors have offered to pick up your assignments and do your weekly chores and errands. Write a letter to one of your friends and explain what you need. Assign each of your friends a necessary task.

# EN MI CUADERNO

Describe your favorite holiday celebration of past years. Be as precise as you can, including time of year, who celebrated this special day with you, who decorated the house and sent the invitations, who came early or late, and if anyone danced, played an instrument, or just talked a lot.

Nombre ______________________ Clase ______________ Fecha ______________

# EN MI CUADERNO

Describe what you and your friends like to do to stay healthy and take care of yourselves. Mention exercise, sleep, and eating habits in your description and tell how you feel when you do and don't stick to your program.

# EN MI CUADERNO

Describe an eventful trip you took. Give many details, telling where you went, with whom, and what happened. You may combine several trips in your description, or write about an imaginary one if you wish.